The Spaces of Irish Drama

The Spaces of Irish Drama
Stage and Place in Contemporary Plays

Helen Heusner Lojek

THE SPACES OF IRISH DRAMA
Copyright © Helen Heusner Lojek, 2011.

All rights reserved.

First published in 2011 by PALGRAVE MACMILLAN® in the United States—a division of St. Martin's Press LLC, 175 Fifth Avenue, New York, NY 10010.

Where this book is distributed in the UK, Europe, and the rest of the world, this is by Palgrave Macmillan, a division of Macmillan Publishers Limited, registered in England, company number 785998, of Houndmills, Basingstoke, Hampshire RG21 6XS.

Palgrave Macmillan is the global academic imprint of the above companies and has companies and representatives throughout the world.

Palgrave® and Macmillan® are registered trademarks in the United States, the United Kingdom, Europe and other countries.

ISBN: 978-0-230-11523-1

Library of Congress Cataloging-in-Publication Data

Lojek, Helen, 1944-
  The spaces of Irish drama : stage and place in contemporary plays / Helen Heusner Lojek.
    p. cm.
  Includes bibliographical references.
  1. English drama—Irish authors—History and criticism. 2. English drama—20th century—History and criticism. 3. Setting (Literature) 4. Place (Philosophy) in literature. 5. Ireland—In literature. I. Title.

PR8789.L59 2011
822'.91099415--dc22   2011013829

A catalogue record of the book is available from the British Library.

Design by Scribe Inc.

First edition: October 2011

For Michael and Meg

Contents

Acknowledgments		ix
Introduction		1
1	Mapping the Territory: Brian Friel's *Translations* (1980)	15
2	Picturing a Changing Landscape: Conor McPherson's *The Weir* (1997)	37
3	Travelling in Place: Marina Carr's *By the Bog of Cats . . .* (1998)	65
4	Exploring Interiors: Frank McGuinness's *Gates of Gold* (2002)	97
Conclusion		127
Notes		135
Bibliography		159
Index		173

Acknowledgments

All scholars depend on work done by their predecessors—a fact of which I am acutely aware. I owe particular debts to the theater scholarship of Christopher Murray and Anthony Roche, whose fine studies of the field are both informative and inspirational. And I have relied heavily on work done by both physical and cultural geographers, whose discussions introduced me to a field quite different than my own.

I owe more particular debts to individuals who generously responded to initial drafts or presentations of segments of this study: Leslie Durham, Charlotte Headrick, and Robert Tracy. Ros Dixon, whose too early death left us all missing a fine and generous colleague, was similarly gracious about providing responses. Emile Pine enabled me to avoid embarrassing factual errors. Students in my Irish drama classes offered the joy of unexpected insights. All flaws, however, are my own.

Patrick Lonergan's *Theatre and Globalization: Irish Drama in the Celtic Tiger Era* did not appear until work on this study was essentially complete, but his insights reinforced many of my understandings, and I have added a variety of references to his work.

Samantha (Sam) Hasey at Palgrave Macmillan was a prompt and efficient provider of editorial advice and sensible suggestions. I am grateful to her.

Boise State University and its Office of Research provided funding without which I could not have accomplished the work necessary for this study. The Boise State University Library tracked down essential materials not in our collection and made them promptly available to me.

As always, I have relied on the family that I love, and that loves me. I am grateful to them all, and to Al, whom I miss terribly.

Introduction

> The stage is a concrete physical place which asks to be filled, and to be given its own concrete language to speak.
>
> —Antonin Artaud, *The Theater and Its Double*

This is a study of space—specifically, a study of stage space as it appears in representative texts by four contemporary Irish playwrights, each with an international reputation, each producing work that continues to shape and influence other dramatists. "Space" in this context refers both to the actual Irish places being represented and to the ways in which the stage is organized to communicate the physicality of the setting as well as the situations of the characters. The focus is on the intersection of two valuable ways of approaching dramatic space: first, the cultural and historical realities that have shaped the playwright and the play's setting; second, the immediate reality of staging that shapes audience reactions. The first approach is largely text-based. The second focuses on performance. In combination, these approaches allow consideration of the extent to which the plays' themes are communicated not only through dialogue but also through nonverbal, nonlinear images provided by the use of stage space.

The plays examined here share thematic concerns that are recurring focuses of many late twentieth-century Irish plays: belonging and not belonging, home and homeland, and an acute awareness of exile in the form of an outsider status that is not necessarily geographic. To belong is to live in accordance with dominant values and mores. Not to belong may mean having been outcast, but it may also indicate defiance and deliberate destabilization of those dominant values. A close connection between Irish issues and Irish drama, cemented in the early years of the Abbey Theatre, persists in contemporary drama, though concern with national independence has ceded its preeminent role to other aspects of how Irish people react to Irish places and spaces.

Eli Rozik's concerns are different than mine, and the only Irish writer he discusses is Beckett, but he has crafted a comprehensive theoretical basis for the sort of study undertaken here. A play script, he suggests, remains both the primary source for performance analysis and a *"deficient text"* for understanding performance. A theater performance is *itself* a text, *"the actual text that a spectator is expected to read, interpret and experience."*[1] Audiences contribute to the creation of a play by "interpreting the signs and signals from the stage"[2] in a transaction roughly parallel to the interaction of reader and text that concerns "reader response" theory. Stage space—the focus here—is only one of the performance-text elements Rozik identifies, but the impossibility of fully separating various elements means that comments appear about other aspects (the implied audience, actions, and language, for example). Performances are ephemeral and elusive, posing challenges to interpretation that seem insurmountable. Despite the fact that both readers and directors often ignore them, stage directions remain the starting point for analysis of stage space. This study seeks to narrow the distance between drama as text and the nonverbal aspects of performance. The play script itself, however, with suggestions about stage space incorporated in stage directions as well as dialogue, remains primary.

In 1984, when of the texts discussed here only Brian Friel's *Translations* had appeared, Seamus Deane identified "a conventional situation from the Irish theatrical tradition—that comic situation in which the dominant (but not necessarily heroic) figure on the stage is a social outsider or outcast who is nevertheless gifted with eloquence." Deane went on to consider the "experience of exile" in Irish plays—exile prompted not by economic or political pressure, but by the demands of individual integrity.[3] Una Chaudhuri has discussed, largely with reference to U.S. drama, a similar pattern, tracing the "dramatic discourse of home" as it is articulated through the principles of "a *victimage of location* and a *heroism of departure*."[4] Amid all the discussion of the Irish diaspora (temporarily lessened by the turn of the twenty-first-century Celtic Tiger), there has been a focus on the strength of those who left Ireland to escape individual, economic, or political pressures and build a life elsewhere. Less attention has been paid to the heroism of staying in place and surviving. Other worlds and the possibility of exile and displacement are evident in the plays discussed here, but persistence, survival, and strong ties to particular Irish locales are also evident, celebrating the Irish homeland and counterbalancing images of the "American wake" or "emigrant's wake" performed for those exiling themselves to other lands.

Any selection of texts for analysis is arbitrary, to a degree. This study makes no pretense of providing a survey of Irish drama. Rather, the focus is on four plays, not because they alone raise issues about place and space in Irish drama, and not because I am arguing that they are the "best" plays of either their authors or Irish drama in general. They are key texts because they are representative texts by important authors and because they use space in varied ways, so that the works illuminate each other. The narrowness of the focus has the advantage of allowing extended specific analysis that results in understandings that can be extended to a range of contemporary plays. A systematic analysis of space in these texts also establishes them in a context broader than that of dramatic studies alone, providing a multidisciplinary lens that lessens the long-standing division between science and the arts. The issues raised in this analysis have a global span, and while I have opted for an extended analysis of a limited number of texts, the same multidisciplinary lens is applicable to a variety of texts from the increasingly global world of contemporary drama. Or, to use another metaphor, spotlighting these works helps train a floodlight on the field of drama—light that should encourage revisiting both these and other texts to discover fresh understandings.

An irony of the contemporary world is that even as globalization and multinational franchises diminish regional particularities, the study of place is gaining increased attention. This study relies not only on the work of theatrical critics like Rozik, Chaudhuri, and Erika Fischer-Lichte but also on a large body of recent work by cultural and physical geographers who examine the implications and constructions of space, whose thinking enriches understanding of drama, and who are cited throughout.[5] It is based on the premise that Antonin Artaud was correct: we cannot subordinate the theatrical to the literary, and drama ought not be studied exclusively as though it were a branch of literature susceptible of understanding in the same way fiction or poetry can be understood. The centrality of performance—including the utilization of space under consideration here—must be recognized. Text is the most constant element in any dramatic production, and text begets (through stage directions and dialogue) the creation of space by particular productions and the reactions to space by particular audiences. Text-based theater dominates Western dramatic traditions. Textual analysis, though, ought not to dominate discussion of a cultural form that relies on convergence between the text and numerous other elements. A hybrid awareness of text and performance clarifies drama's essentials, and the application of understandings culled from geographers facilitates an awareness that understanding issues of space enriches enjoyment and comprehension both of drama and of the wide world we inhabit. Noting how characters in these plays relate to space illuminates our relationships to space as well as theirs.

The argument for allowing theater to speak in concrete terms and for a less exclusive reliance on textual criticism is neither simple nor unanswerable. T. S. Eliot, for example, both lamented the "instability of any art . . . which depends upon representation by performers"⁶ and, decades later (after he had written *Murder in the Cathedral*, *The Family Reunion*, and *The Cocktail Party*), developed an astute understanding of theatrical realities.⁷ Marina Carr, whose work is the focus of Chapter 3, has argued that plays *should* be treated as text: "I've read far more plays than I've ever seen on stage."⁸ In general, academics have concurred with Carr, concentrating on text over performance with an approach that "flattens [drama's] multiple sensory appeals into a text to be read."⁹

I have sought both to value the written word and to couple textual analysis with consideration of how the use of stage space shapes understanding of characters and their worlds. Audiences see as well as hear, and each sense affects perceptions by the other. Even if we encounter plays exclusively as text, reading with the "mind's eye" brings us closer to realizing the impact of nonverbal, nonlinear performance elements. To note them is not to opt for an alternative approach to textual analysis but to couple attention to text with awareness that playwrights do not select dramatic sites arbitrarily and that stage spaces are not casual background, but deliberate reinforcements of important themes. While no study of space can illuminate all aspects of either text or production, considerations of space provide a lens through which to see things that might otherwise be missed.

Recent reinterpretations of such classic dramatic texts as Shakespeare's *The Taming of the Shrew* and *The Merchant of Venice* provide ample evidence that productions are rooted in time as well as space. While recognizing those interconnections, I have chosen to concentrate on dramatic space—the space of the stage set itself, the offstage space described in dialogue, and the geographic space represented by the set and described in the dialogue. On the one hand, stage space varies from venue to venue and is a matter of practical concern to particular productions: How large is the stage? How technically elaborate? How far from the audience? How flexible in allowing for entrances and exits? How does the relationship between the theater building and the surrounding urban or rural space influence theatergoers? With luck, dealing with the opportunities and challenges of stage space in this sense can lead to stunningly imaginative and effective productions. It can also, of course, yield failures that sap the energy of a play. Occasionally my fascination with such practical production issues of stage space will be clear. Primarily, though, the focus here is on the other hand of stage space: the production of a shaped environment that illuminates not only the world of the play but also the contemporary world outside the theater. Each of those worlds informs the other, since the relationship between theater and the social reality of theatergoers is fundamentally dialectical. As Fischer-Lichte has explained, the characteristic of theater that sets it off from all other cultural systems is that "in the act of spectating [an audience gains] distance from the culture depicted and from itself . . . Theater becomes a model of cultural reality in which the spectators confront the meaning of that reality."[10]

Richard Hornby describes terminology as "a nagging problem," particularly when it is necessary to distinguish between *drama* and *theater*, or between *playscript* and *play*.[11] And Gay McAuley has noted the "terminological minefield" resulting from the absence of a shared vocabulary that allows us to distinguish between "stage, set, and the fictional place(s) represented." Unlike the commonly agreed on difference between "character" and "actor," he argues, terminology for space blurs rather than sharpens the precision with which we are able to discuss the difference between stage space and the places being represented.[12] The linguistic challenges are multiplied when the "fictional place" being represented makes a clear reference to an actual, geographical place, as so often happens in Irish theater. I have sought always to make clear which aspects of script, performance, place, and space are my focus in particular sections.

Henry Lefebvre's theory of social space argues that no space is simply "there"—that all spaces are imaginative "productions" that represent (through such material means as architecture, urban planning, and civil engineering) social and political realities.[13] This study focuses on dramatic representations of the interior and exterior spaces of home and homeland as equally imaginative products. I have seen productions of all the plays discussed, sometimes more than one production. My interest, though, is less in what productions did and more in what the text suggests they might or ought to do, those textual indications of how playwrights have sought to describe a created environment in which to locate their created characters and actions. Audiences understand that the stage space before them is not "real," but rather a necessarily artificial visual representation of the playwright's imagined reality. The translation of space involved in the movement from observable outside space to equally observable constructed stage space involves both a conventional renegotiation of physical details and a shared sense of the "reality" of imagined or constructed space.

Objects on the stage reveal the interaction of the world outside the stage with the world represented on the stage. What audiences literally see on stage is shaped by stage directions and dialogue. What audiences imaginatively see in the offstage world is shaped by dialogue.[14] In considering this interaction I am concerned primarily with objects described in the script. Such objects may, of course, have been incorporated as part of the collaborative vision (writer, director, scenic designer) of the first production. Nevertheless, the incorporation of particular objects in the text indicates that the playwright has accepted them as appropriate representations of the play's vision of the "real" world. As a whole, the dramatic space incorporates a representational strategy—naturalistic or abstract or something between those extremes—by which a playwright attempts to focus audience attention on a particular vision of the world.

The spaces of home and homeland in the plays considered here are inevitably framed by the larger issue of Ireland's geographical space, which has long been a contested area—colonial, postcolonial, possessed, dispossessed, preserved, exploited. Awareness of borders is acute on the island, where institutions and individuals wrestle with conflicting demands, and where internationalism sailed in the wake of devolution. Recent studies like *Space and the Irish Cultural Imagination* (2001) and *Ireland: Space, Text, Time* (2005)[15] examine over a sweep of time issues considered here in relation to four plays. The 2010 "Ireland, Landscapes" conference organized by the French Society for Irish Studies at the University of Nantes is further indication of an increasing focus on issues of space in Irish culture and literature.

Playwrights considered here vary widely in many ways, but they and their audiences share a common contemporary understanding of stage space that facilitates the focus on home and belonging. That understanding is sharply different from such earlier shared understandings as the Elizabethan attachment to hierarchal stage space, or the medieval use of wagons, or the Greek reliance on amphitheaters. That understanding is also sharply different from understandings of other spaces that are equally, in Victor Turner's phrase, "liminal."[16] Generally, rituals (baptism or marriage, for example) represent a perceived change in the lives of the participants; spectators of the ritual are likely to have arrived sharing the world view (illuminated by the ritual) that participants have now accepted. In theater, characters may change, yet we do not ordinarily expect that the actors will change. Or, if the actors change, it is likely to have been during the script exploration and rehearsal rather than during a performance. By contrast, many playwrights, actors, and even spectators hope that audiences will be changed by a production. Playgoers, then, have a different relation to the stage space than observers of weddings, and there may be a gap between the concept of identity presented on stage and the concept of identity that predominates in the audience. Both Nicholas Grene and Patrick Lonergan have noted the tendency of Irish drama to "look to social margins for its setting,"[17] so that "representations of Ireland were always presented for an audience presupposed to be homogenized, metropolitan, and inherently different from the

Irish being presented."[18] The plays considered in this study are all products of a complex society. Their likely Irish audiences, though, are generally homogeneous. One result is that audiences are asked to consider not so much their own lives as their own notions of what it means to be "Irish" and at home on the island.

With only minor exceptions, these plays rely on single sets that are compatible with proscenium arch stages. There are many reasons for this reliance, not the least of which is the frequency with which Irish productions tour and the economic realities of Irish theater venues, which often have neither the funds nor the technical capacity to accommodate set changes easily. The common use of single sets has resulted in reliance on sets that may be used to frame complex dramatic realities. One result is that audiences in the darkened and defined space of relatively traditional theaters encounter actors in the equally defined space of single sets. While such defined spaces may initially seem restrictive, I believe that the use of stage space in these plays allows theater to mimic modernism's shifts of attention from exterior to interior realities, and the constraints of naturalism become opportunities to combine attention to external realities of home with awareness of personal, interior, psychological realities of belonging or not belonging, feeling at home or feeling at odds with homeland.

The playwrights considered here also share an understanding of stage space. Though some contemporary Irish playwrights use found space or approach street drama, for example, I have not dealt with them. Because the playwrights considered here use fairly conventional stage space, the often-mocked Irish peasant cottage and its kitchen (favored settings for Irish drama early in the last century) are always a referent, though usually an unstated referent, simply part of the audience's mental picture gallery of Irish stage homes.

Discussing Northern Irish poetry, Seamus Heaney observed: "Each person in Ulster lives first in the Ulster of the actual present, and then in one or other Ulster of the mind."[19] Heaney's essay makes clear his recognition that the "strain of being in two places at once" is not unique to Ulster poets.[20] Certainly that strain is evident in the plays considered here, which are products of a changed and changing Ireland. The ubiquitous and familiar stage Irish cottage is important as a mental image because it represents a built space of home that has long disappeared as a major feature of the Ireland of the actual present, but that persists in the Ireland of the mind.

Dramatic and cultural representations of the Irish cottage are generally recognized as *created* in the sense of *imagined*. The cottage was transformed into a place of authenticity and purity, simultaneously "real" enough to be recognized and ideal enough to be longed for. There is less awareness that exterior natural space is as created as buildings or stage space. Partly exterior space must be seen as created because "virgin," unmodified land is difficult to find anywhere in Europe or North America, but it is also true that even when the world's physical realities stay relatively constant, mental images of them can change radically, just as different individuals looking at the same sign (or the same individual looking at the sign at different times) may find different meanings. The Irish bogs, for example, which were once seen as "unimproved" wasteland where "unregenerate" rebels could evade English authorities, later became a natural resource that could be usefully mined for commercial fuel development. Bogs are now often seen as areas of stunning beauty that should be preserved (as they have preserved artifacts from Irish history) and protected from the commercial exploitation that strips and degrades their natural wonders. Attitudes toward and mental images of the bogs have changed more than the bogs themselves, at least where those bogs have been left unmined for turf. Ultimately, "reality" and "image" cannot be untangled, and that tangle affects the ways in which the exterior physical spaces of home and homeland are represented on stage. It also means that production of space on stage is a miniature version of production of space all around us every day.

It is now over a decade since Declan Hughes wondered what Irish playwrights were doing "stuck down in the country being Irish with themselves" and argued against setting Irish plays in communities "where everyone talks and thinks the same and holds values in common."[21] Plays considered in this study are products of an Ireland in which most people do not live in cottages or hold values in common. Three of the four plays are indeed set "down in the country," but that setting is used to reveal differences and changes, not to establish an idyllic rural Ireland. Rather, these plays reflect what Eamonn Jordan has termed "a nation that has abandoned its post-colonial narrative."[22] Brian Friel, the oldest of the playwrights considered here, was born in 1929; Conor McPherson, the youngest, was born in 1971. Friel was born in County Tyrone, Northern Ireland; McGuinness was born in Donegal, a county adjacent to Tyrone but part of the Republic; Carr was born in the Midlands County Offaly; McPherson was born in Dublin. Their varied ages and experiences provide varied lenses through which themes of belonging are examined and stage space is created.

This study is not a full theoretical analysis of stage space, or even of stage space in contemporary Irish drama. I focus on four plays, each by a major contemporary playwright and each designed for the institutional spaces of official culture. I mention only in passing the questions of how particular performance venues affect the drama, and of how particular performers use the space in particular productions. When Samuel Beckett shaped the abstract patterns of *Quad*, he was deliberately nonrepresentational, allowing pattern to triumph over particular stage space—an imposition as arbitrary as the laying out of streets in grids, or the division of land in the western United States into geometric units regardless of topography. For numerous plays, however, the production venues have mattered greatly.[23] When Brian Friel's *Translations* premiered in Derry's Guildhall, for example, audience awareness of the building's political and cultural importance influenced reaction to the play presented in that unconventional theater venue.[24]

When Frank McGuinness's *Gates of Gold* was premiered in the theater founded by the men who inspired the playwright's characters, audiences inevitably connected the action on stage with the physical space in which they were seated. If they remembered that the Gate's theater space was originally part of the Rotunda Hospital (Dublin's Lying-In Hospital), they may also have made a connection with the characters' discussion of children. When Charabanc Theatre Company (1983–95) toured its productions to parish halls and leisure centers, audience awareness that theater was coming to them rather than asking them to come to high-culture venues mattered greatly. When *Convictions* used Belfast's Crumlin Road Courthouse and Gaol as a venue through which audiences literally moved, it was impossible to escape both the echoes of the building's painful history and an awareness that this change of function for the building might be a reason for hope. When J. B. Keane's *Sive* and *The Field* were performed in the Abbey Theatre, audience members who knew that the Abbey had originally rejected the plays saw the productions through a particular lens. In general, audiences at the Abbey know the theater has had a role in the history of Irish nationalism; that knowledge may, in fact, be part of the reason tourists flock to the Abbey. In the 1980s, when the Diceman walked Grafton Street in drag as an advertisement for *The Rocky Horror Picture Show*, his mime was perceived differently than it would have been in an enclosed area with a self-selected audience. Live art and street art embrace the freedom of unconventional spaces, often choosing to share space with audiences who may not have chosen to be spectators. Cyberspace has become a sort of placeless venue that exaggerates what Beckett often achieved in his film and television work.

Such aspects of theater and stage space, however, lie outside the concerns that animate this study. The places in these plays are specific. The characters in these plays generally opt to remain in those specific places, whatever the difficulties of home and homeland. Considering the plays in the order of their creation provides a perspective that moves from rural western Ireland to the urban east of Dublin, from mid-nineteenth century to generally twentieth century. The outsiders in *Translations* are the intrusive British army, but the play's Irish characters consider exile, which would make them outsiders. Outsiders in *The Weir* are both the foreign tourists who do not appear on stage and the Dubliner who moves to a rural area. In *By the Bog of Cats* . . . the focus is on one of Ireland's domestic outsiders, a member of the Travelling community who is an outsider despite her deep roots in the area. And in *Gates of Gold* audiences are presented with another inherently outsider group—gays, who are other regardless of country of birth. What none of these plays illustrates is a pattern of Irish characters following Stephen Dedalus's decision to leave Ireland in order to learn "away from home and friends what the heart is and what it feels."[25] Rather, characters in these plays generally opt to remain in the Irish places where they feel they belong and where they hope others will accept them as Irish insiders. There are challenges in going, hardships in exile whether it is self-imposed or not. There are equal challenges in staying and making a home in a place where acceptance is not easy. The heroism of departures is matched in these plays by the heroism of staying in place. The interfaces between staying and going, between belonging and not belonging provide spaces where individuals may be most alive.

 I have resisted the temptation to force the plays into a simplistic thematic line, opting to vary the approach in accordance with the text under consideration and utilizing theories of geography and stage space that seem most likely to open up particular texts. Bringing various perspectives to bear on the ways stage spaces are used to represent the places of home provides clues that open up the dramas' themes and implications. It also provides clues to the ways all individuals relate to the spaces of home and homeland.

CHAPTER 1

Mapping the Territory

Brian Friel's *Translations* (1980)

> Order must be derived from significant experience and not from arbitrary abstractions and concepts as represented on maps and plans.
> —Edward Relph, *Place and Placelessness*

Act Two of Brian Friel's *Translations* (1980) opens with Yolland (the English orthographer) and Owen (the Irish translator) bending over a large, blank map of the surrounding Donegal area. Boundaries are being drawn on the map, and their task is to translate the Irish names used by residents into English. Act Three also opens with the map stretched across the stage space. After the map is folded away in Act Three, Maire kneels on the floor and "draws" with her finger the map of Norfolk that Yolland had drawn on the sand for her the night before. Friel specifies that Maire is drawing in precisely the spot where the literal map had been only moments before. Like Shakespeare's map in *King Lear*, Friel's map (center stage for over half the play) provides powerful visual signals of themes that also dominate the play's language and action.[1] As if to bolster these visual images, Friel's characters apply spatial terms to temporal and linguistic realities, talking about "a linguistic *contour* which no longer matches the *landscape* of . . . fact," and describing the translation as "an *eviction* of sorts" that amounts to "Something . . . being *eroded*." Place-names have "*roots*,"[2] and "boundaries" are as often cultural as physical. Friel's title reminds us of the importance and limitations of language; the play's references to geographic space remind us of the importance and limitations of cartography; and Friel uses stage space to "map" character relations, repositioning characters and reconfiguring set pieces as the action develops over time. The resulting visual images both reveal and reinforce important aspects of the set, which at various times serves as both home and hedge school, focusing attention on who belongs and who does not and on the tangled relationships of insiders and outsiders.

Questions of time have been extensively analyzed in relation to the play's consideration of colonial and postcolonial space. That body of previous analysis informs and underlies my focus on the ways in which the stage space itself serves to underscore themes. The map's powerful presence requires a more-nuanced approach to the play than that suggested by Friel's contention that "the play has to do with language and only language."[3] The set itself, and transformations in it, shape reactions in ways that, while audiences may not be thoroughly conscious of them, are crucial to the focus on time, space, belonging, and home: *Translations* takes place in a hedge school specifically described as converted space: "a disused barn or hay-shed or byre. Along the back wall are the remains of five or six stalls . . . where cows were once milked and bedded . . . Around the room are broken and forgotten implements" (1). This room, full of emblems of the past, is the home of the schoolmaster and his son. Shortly after the play begins, though, the characters reorganize the space for class, placing stools, books, and slates for the students. When visitors arrive, students remove the school items to restore the emphasis on living space. The transformations evident in the set—from barn to living space to schoolroom to living space—are spatial instances of social changes as radical as the changes tracked in the contrast of languages (Greek, Latin, Irish, and English), and many of them take place before the audience's eyes. The hedge school reveals itself as converted space that is susceptible to further change, and actions in Act One reinforce awareness that even when the walls of a structure remain the same the cultural importance of the enclosed space can—and perhaps inevitably will—change dramatically. Arrangements of stalls or schoolbooks or laundry lines help the audience decode the play's rearranged space. The small modifications are significant. Like Chekhov's use of changed settings in such plays as *The Sea Gull* and *The Cherry Orchard*, Friel's shifting set provides an early visual signal that the world of *Translations* is unstable.[4] Because Irish theater has a long tradition of establishing a home (usually a rural cottage) as a metaphor for homeland, and because hedge schools were and are so tightly connected to Irish linguistic, political, and religious resistance to British colonialism, the set itself suggests the instability not just of this small town but of the island as a whole.

The hedge school space functions alternately and sometimes simultaneously as personal or domestic space and as public or communal space. Within that space Friel regularly reconfigures relationships among the characters. Doalty's arrival with a surveyor's pole he has lifted from the British army sappers charged with mapping the area is an intrusion of foreign instruments associated with foreign ways of understanding. The entrances of Hugh and Owen realign the communal structures. The appearance of Yolland and Lancey in the hedge school mimics the exterior invasion of the British army, and the schoolroom is altered accordingly, emerging as a place where communication between the English and the Irish may at least begin. Unlike the shifting space of the hedge school, which may be reconfigured to serve different purposes while remaining a familiar structure, the new school will be a purpose-built space suitable to the standardized reordering of education and language that it will house and that the British expect will be permanent.

The Irish stage home as a familiar metaphor for the Irish homeland hints that this dysfunctional family may reveal a dysfunctional culture and allows for additional resonances associated with space. The play is framed by the homecoming of one son (who no longer really belongs in Ballybeg and whose name is as unstable as the home and homeland from which he comes) and the departure from home of the other son (who will be an outsider in whatever place he ends up, even though it will be in Ireland). The father comes home from a much closer space (the pub), and soon he will depart for the not-too-distant space of the new school, where it is difficult to imagine that he will feel at home. Yolland thinks he can feel at home in Ballybeg. Maire wants to leave. The British army arrives for a clearly temporary stay. Questions of belonging and not belonging, outsider and insider, integration and reintegration, home and away emerge without being resolved. Friel's use of stage space provides a picture of intrusion and departure, focusing attention on what it means to belong.

The Ordnance Survey's plotting of Donegal's geographic features on the two-dimensional "reality" of a map represents a rearrangement of exterior space parallel to the rearrangements of interior space. In nineteenth-century Donegal, mapping was a different way of understanding territory. The Irish did not begin to make maps until the seventeenth century, and the Irish language of Friel's characters does not even include a word for *map*.[5] Friel's parallel emphases on language and cartography reflect two of the sources he has identified as important impetuses for the writing of *Translations*: George Steiner's 1975 *After Babel: Aspects of Language and Translation* and J. H. Andrews's 1975 *A Paper Landscape: The Ordnance Survey in Nineteenth-Century Ireland*. Steiner's influence on Friel's play has been extensively analyzed.[6] Andrews's description of the historical nineteenth-century mapping of Ireland had an equally potent influence on *Translations*. Both Lancey and Yolland have names found in Andrews's account, for example.[7] Furthermore, the notion of a "paper landscape," with all the tensions and ambiguities bound up in the term, helped to shape Friel's consideration of space.[8] The pain and significance of translating place names is revealed primarily in dialogue. The centrality of the map provides a visual focus, drawing attention to the sharp division between "old" and "new" ways of understanding space. As Declan Kiberd has pointed out, mapping is a "form of translation" parallel to linguistic translation because both "assert one's power" over "the oral memory of the natives."[9] Ireland in the 1970s, when Friel was writing, had for decades been obsessed with the creation and erasure of borders, and ultimately the implications of the map and mapping spread beyond the time period of the play to include the Ireland of both the nineteenth and the twentieth centuries.

The room's single window—like the window in Synge's *The Playboy of the Western World*—is an important feature, allowing characters to bring the wider world in by gazing out and describing what they see. Simultaneously, the window separates them from this wider world. What the characters describe is almost never the land's geographic features. Rather, they describe what humans are doing in the space. For them, landscape is the setting for human activities. They do not share the (admittedly vague) awareness of characters in *The Weir* that landscape has a history and that people have changed it. Nor do they share the affection of Hester in *By the Bog of Cats . . .* for a relatively unchanged landscape.[10] Descriptions of the outside world in *Translations* are not always accompanied by a gaze through the window and are not always focused on the immediately surrounding area. Owen describes his journey home from Dublin to Omagh to Ballybeg, signaling a steady northwest movement from a densely populated urban area to a small rural community. Hugh describes going to battle in 1798, marching 23 miles "across the fresh green land" (81) and back again. When he tells Hugh how to find the priest's house (a house Hugh could probably find blindfolded), Owen emphasizes the changes in spatial understanding by referring to the landmarks with their new English names and asking whether his father will recognize them with those designations.

The descriptions of journeys convey a feeling of movement, nearly always movement through rural space, into the hedge school. There are also references to Nova Scotia, India, France, America, and England. The small and particular space of the hedge school, then, is carefully situated in Donegal (the area being mapped), Ireland (which contains Donegal), Great Britain (which seeks greater control over Ireland), and the wider British colonial world. And the known nineteenth-century English-speaking world is framed by constant references to the classical worlds of Greece and Rome, the spaces emphasized at the close of the play. Eden as a metaphor for Ireland also occurs twice, a recasting of Shakespearean and Spenserian uses of Eden as a metaphor for England.

The reality that Donegal has different meanings for different observers is evident not only in Yolland's and Manus's contrasting views of local weather but also in Maire's linking of "the best harvest in living memory" with the blisters on her hands and a desire never to see a similar harvest (8). Lancey sees Donegal as space that needs to be mapped for purposes of civic and military control. Yolland conflates Donegal's landscape with a viable culture that he might be able to join. The Donegalers see it as a complex amalgam of land, homeland, and history. Gerry Smyth describes the Irish cultural revival (which, he argues, continued until the end of the twentieth century) as one in which "history was the primary conceptual consideration . . . History was . . . the record of emplaced humanity . . . apprehensible with reference to environment and land."[11] It is that understanding of the symbiotic relationship of people and place that the mapping process challenges.

Bernhard Klein has described this "confrontation between two competing claims to the land" in early modern England and Ireland: "The abstract result of a survey—the geometric outline—requires the cartographer to move beyond a sense of land as a local and social space, deeply immersed in regional custom, that defies its translation into a set of mathematical data."[12] The sixteenth century's somewhat schizophrenic juxtapositions (found in Spenser and other commentators) of images of Ireland as Eden and images of Irish "destruction and savagery" were no doubt, in part, attempts "to make Ireland an attractive option for new . . . settlers"[13] while preserving the implication of English superiority. Similar contrasts were equally evident in the nineteenth century, when the play is set, and again in the twentieth century, when the play was written and when Ireland was deemed both tourist mecca and terrorist enclave. In the seventeenth century, tensions involved in the competing claims to land resulted in the murder of an English cartographer at the hands of Donegal residents whose territory he was mapping. The inhabitants, a contemporary reported, "took off his head, because they would not have their country discovered."[14] That case seems close to the disappearance of Friel's Yolland, but Yolland's fate is never clear and motives for doing him harm are both personal and political—a tangle of factors familiar in twentieth-century Ireland.

Such real and dramatic resistance to English mapping of Irish territory is only one of the resistances, many with implications for space, reflected in this play. The hedge school itself is a place of resistance to English language education, and it is under threat from the coming of the national schools. Hugh's suggestion that the Irish "overlook" England to focus on Greece and Rome is connected, of course, to Irish Catholic resistance to English Protestantism, but Hugh's description gives the linguistic and religious resistance a territorial focus. The British army is employed in an effort to control Irish territory, which was widely regarded as the site of rebellious attitudes toward British rule. All these are efforts at standardization—standard language, standard schooling, standard religion, and standard ways of understanding territory. There are, then, ironies involved in the fact that only within the hedge school are the English and the Irish able to communicate with each other, however imperfectly, while violence remains outside. Once the standardization is complete, communication will in some ways be easier, though the shift to English as the standard (like the shift to maps as a standard way of understanding territory) represents a loss as well as a gain.

Friel's hedge school exists as more than the omphalos of the play's wider world. It is also stage space created within an Irish dramatic tradition that has been powerful since the start of the Abbey Theatre. The ubiquity of the peasant kitchen as a setting for decades of Irish plays has been often noted and almost as often chuckled about. Its serious implications can be found in Friel's hedge school, which, while not a kitchen, is clearly peasant and continues the familiar dramatic trope of home as nation. Friel has deviated from the peasant kitchen norm by imagining a converted space that is not really a kitchen, and by establishing its womanless family of inhabitants. The wife or mother figure central to so many stereotypical dramatic kitchens[15] is missing here, and the hopeless, often literally mute yearnings of Maire and Sarah make her absence particularly poignant. Nevertheless, Friel's peasant set and cast represent, in part, the extent to which Irish drama has defined itself in opposition to establishment English drama,[16] just as hedge schools developed in opposition to legal, establishment educational spaces and practices. Plenty of non-peasant Irish plays have been written, but Irish plays set in the rural west (which artist Paul Henry called "the very soul of Ireland"[17]) are unstated assertions that people and places need not be aristocratic or middle-class or even English in order to be taken seriously. In this play Friel's Irish characters are poor, powerless, and often only marginally literate. They are often bawdy and funny. What they are not is simple comic relief. In *Translations* serious issues are not presented in the lives of privileged, sophisticated individuals. Multiple elaborate sets, hierarchal stages, the King's English—all yield to an emphasis on the significance of lives lived on the economic, cultural, social, and geographic margins of the British Isles.

Friel's use of Latin and Greek, particularly Jimmy Jack's recitations from Homer's *Odyssey* and Virgil's *Georgics*, underscores the significance of ordinary people. Jimmy hints that the rough exterior concealing the nobility of the Greek hero (whom both he and Hugh refer to as "Ulysses") is like his own rough exterior, and he suggests that Virgil's "black soil" is like Donegal's. Like Hugh's insistence that Ireland has more in common with the classics than with the English, such parallels constitute a kind of insistence that the lives of these Donegal residents are worthy of attention. Seamus Heaney made a similar connection between place and language: "I like to remember that Dante was very much a man of a particular place, that his great poem is full of intimate placings and place-names, and that . . . he is recognized by his local speech."[18] An emphasis on rural Ireland as the "true" Ireland was part of Irish nationalism, both before and after independence. Distrust of urban areas, the seats of colonial power, is evident not only on the Abbey Theatre stage but also in the Republic's 1937 constitution and its self-image. (In Northern Ireland, where Friel's roots lie, antiurban feeling is generally less.) *Translations*, situated in Ireland's border region, occupies space that facilitates interrogating the ubiquitous romantic image of rural Ireland.

If Friel's set and peasant characters can be seen as instances of the Irish tendency to assert an identity in opposition to the stifling presence of the English colonizer,[19] it is equally important to recognize the play's rejection of the romantic Irish revival notion that "the" peasant (who belonged) was purer, more spiritual, indeed more Irish than urban West Britons (who did not belong). As Edward Hirsch has pointed out, the romantic "overturning" of the negative English stage Irishman figure resulted in an "imaginary Irish peasant" whose qualities were equally far from reality.[20] Friel's Donegalers are neither monolithic nor idealized. They are often less articulate, crueler, and more ignorant than the romantic image. Synge had earlier interrogated the myth in *The Playboy of the Western World* (1907), portraying common peasant cruelties in combination with the "fiery and magnificent, and tender" popular imagination of Ireland and the "rich and living" language of the country's rural residents.[21] Magnificent imagination (unless we count Jimmy Jack) is in scant supply in *Translations*, and the language seems living but hardly rich. Furthermore, at least two characters are eager to reverse Synge's move into the "authentic" West by heading east to Dublin (or further) or west to America. The Englishman Yolland, who knows least about rural Ireland, is most enamored of the romantic image of the folk and the West. The Irishman Owen, for whom the area was once home, most clearly sees both the outsider's overly romantic desire to belong in Donegal and the need to counter that romanticism before it damages lives.[22]

Hugh, the schoolmaster who rules the play's mutable interior space with an authority that is unmatched and largely unchallenged, represents a direct counter to romantic notions of the Irish West. His character owes much to the image of hedge school teachers presented in P. J. Dowling's 1935 *The Hedge Schools of Ireland* (extracts from which appeared in the first production's program).[23] Hugh displays an impressive familiarity with classical languages and texts, claims to be a poet, and has a true linguist's fondness for etymologies. He is also frequently drunk, generally reliant on the unappreciated son he has lamed, and always overly impressed with himself. He contends that the English language is "particularly suited" for the "purposes of commerce" (23)[24] and explains to Yolland that he does not know Wordsworth's poetry because "we're not familiar with your literature . . . We feel closer to the warm Mediterranean. We tend to overlook your island" (50). Such episodes—like Hugh's pompous attempts to be hospitable when the English arrive—are both comic and ironic, allowing us to laugh both at the English assumption of superiority and at the Irish counterassumption that a "rich language" and "rich literature" make them a "spiritual people" despite their lack of material wealth (50). It is the physical space of Friel's play that sets us up to notice such implications. The peasant home in the West of Ireland is such a standard dramatic locale that the rise of curtain and lights will evoke standard reactions from the audience. The play goes on to query those standard reactions. Hugh may be "overlooking" England in a cultural sense, but the English are overlooking *his* island in a scientific sense as they map it in ways that suggest they are looking down from above. *Translations* allows the cultural and scientific understandings to bounce off each other, creating a nonverbal dialogue.

The red coats of the invading soldiers contrast with the dress of locals, and their powerful equipment and language disrupt norms that are never restored. Neither education nor the vernacular nor (it seems likely) the agrarian livelihood will remain unchanged. One of the more powerful changes involves the way people conceive of space. An adumbrated and perhaps degraded but nonetheless powerful version of the ancient Irish tradition of *dinnseanchas* persists in the world of *Translations*. Seamus Heaney has described *dinnseanchas* as a uniting of place-names and events into a sort of "mythical etymology." The Irish, Heaney noted, recognize that they are "inhabitants not just of a geographical country but of a country of the mind."[25] Traditionally, Irish realities of time and space were—and perhaps still are—united in place-names.

As Matthew Johnson has pointed out, the significance of local maps is that they find "a space in the widening gap between the landscape and what it means," replacing "cultural meaning" with "utilitarian" descriptions that attempt neutrality: "Demand for maps derived ultimately from the shift in the understanding of space, from space as subjectively experienced as a locale of social relations to space as objectively measured as a form of commodity... [Maps] are opposed to subjective folk experience of the landscape... [and to] popular terminology as revealed in place-names."[26] Modern understandings may, to a degree, be moving back to an earlier notion of landscape, a word with roots in Dutch and German words "signif[ying] a unit of human occupation."[27] The European Landscape Convention, for example, has defined landscape as "an area, as perceived by people, whose character is the result of the action and interaction of natural and/or human factors."[28] Friel's sappers, however, are concentrating on the scientific measurement of space that their government has deemed most useful, and that they believe will enable them to exert control over the landscape and over the Irish who inhabit that landscape. Their measuring mentality—like the absence of geographic descriptions when residents look through the window—represents a clearly partial understanding of landscape.

The play's sharpest recognition of the power and the problems of *dinnseanchas* as a way of understanding space comes in Owen's consideration of *Tobair Vree*, a name that no longer matches the place it seeks to designate, because the history is lost to common memory. *Tobair Vree* literally means "Brian's well," and Brian Friel's choice of this particular "outgrown" name—like his indication that Hugh had marched only as far as Glenties, where Friel spent boyhood summers—seems a personal reference. Owen, who has been hired because of his skill with the Irish language and his familiarity with the area, poses the question whether to preserve the name Tobair Vree and thus "keep piety with a man long dead, long forgotten, his name 'eroded' beyond recognition, whose trivial little story nobody in the parish remembers" (53, quotation marks in original). Similar linguistic transformations are evident in the repeated mentions of *Bun na hAbhann*. *Abha*, Owen tells Yolland, means *river* (39). What he does not say is that *Abha* (or the Welsh *Afta*) mutated into the English *Avon*; Shakespeare's River Avon, then, has a redundant place-name (River River) because its etymology is lost to common memory.[29]

The complexity of preserving or abandoning place-names with forgotten etymologies is also evident in Andrews's description of John O'Donovan, hired by the historical Survey to help with lexicography and orthography. Ranked "high among the greatest Irish scholars of all time," O'Donovan "was skeptical about the value and durability of much minor nomenclature." In fact, reports Andrews, O'Donovan "found himself investigating a name that the local people had never heard of until it was told them by his own colleagues." Describing challenges facing the historical orthographers, Andrews emphasizes the "awkward problems" posed by Ireland, where indigenous authorities, place-names, and even spellings varied, and where both spellings and pronunciations were strange to English eyes and ears[30] (a strangeness illustrated in Friel's play by the English mishearing of *Owen* as *Roland*). A conservative attitude toward changes indicated "respect for Ireland's cultural heritage" and the need to "facilitate the continued use of old documents in modern legal proceedings"; London's frustration, though, is evident in an 1836 note sent to one orthographer: "strange admission that you can give 'no positive information' as to the name of a place surveyed by you!"[31]

The play posits a persistent close relationship between the Irish people and their places. Owen, for example, identifies Sarah not by occupation, and less by family name than by place: "Of course! From Bun na hAbhann!" (30). Hugh's difficulty marching farther than Glenties is balanced against the willingness of the English to march through both Ireland and India. It is not, of course, a simple issue. Manus does leave Ballybeg, and Maire's eagerness to go either to American or to England is balanced against Yolland's eagerness to stay in a country he does not really understand. Mention of the potato famine (whose major impact did not hit Ireland until more than a decade later) heightens emphasis on central questions: Who belongs in Ballybeg? Is it a place to move *to* or *away from*? Yolland's understanding that the Irish are closely tied to their space underlies his application of the "linguistic landscape" metaphor previously used by Hugh and derived from George Steiner's *After Babel*. A map, after all, is a language of sorts—a way of organizing information.

Translations' most powerful focus on ways of conceiving space comes by way of the set pieces associated with maps or mapmaking. In Act One, Maire is studying the map of America, and when the students scuttle to their places in anticipation of Hugh's arrival, it is the atlas she reaches for to demonstrate her academic seriousness. Here, as with his mention of the potato famine, Friel may be allowing thematic usefulness to trump strict historical accuracy. His mention of hedge school practices, though, generally follows historical accounts,[32] and Dowling reports that geography (in addition to reading, writing, the classics, and bookkeeping) were standard hedge school subjects. There were Irish geographies. Whether there would also have been an atlas with a map of America—and what language it would have been written in—is less clear,[33] but Maire's atlas and Doalty's arrival with the surveyors' theodolite begin the focus on space and maps carried out in the use of the large map in Acts Two and Three. When in Act Three Maire laments her failure to get her geography done and traces with her finger an outline of the map of England that Yolland had drawn "on the wet strand" (78) before he disappears, her finger tracing is one of the play's inescapable visual reminders of surveying and mapmaking. Yolland's map would have been quickly washed out by waves, but it persists in Maire's mind and suggests an altered perception of space. The visual reminders emphasize the fact that the Irish lore of places embodied in *dinnseanchas* is being replaced by a two-dimensional, reproducible rendering aimed at providing all viewers with comparable understandings of space they may never have visited. Friel's play, set in 1833, illustrates the shift in thinking about place that Nicholas Entrikin has identified in late nineteenth-century debates between the "decentered universalism" of Enlightenment scholars and the "centered particularism" of their critics—critics who argued that "universal values are never universal, because (in the words of Kant) they always bring with them a clump of the native soil from the national sphere, a sphere that no individual can completely leave behind."[34]

Cartography involves an effort to assert understanding and control over the natural world. It also involves an assertion that a single method of understanding adequately fits all regions. The understanding provided by maps is, of course, at least partially a fiction. A person examining contour lines on a map understands elevation differently than a person who has walked up the represented hill. And a person who climbs knowing that family members have climbed that same hill for centuries has yet another understanding. Finding the way by maps is significantly different than finding the way by use of landmarks. The current shift back from maps to landmarks, as revealed in the sorts of directions obtained from MapQuest or automobile navigators, is a reminder of the sharpness of the difference. In *Translations*, though, geographic and human features of the landscape are being replaced by maps emphasizing proprietary boundaries that may, or may not, follow the landscape's features and that are unlikely to reflect the understandings of those who have long belonged to the area.

The appearance of the concrete implements of mapmaking brings an inescapably exterior process into the hedge school interior. The play's one exterior scene (which requires not a set change, but merely a dimming of the lights and an engagement of the audience's imagination) is a love scene with no specific reminders of mapmaking, though Maire and Yolland are certainly crossing metaphoric boundaries. With the exception of that one brief exterior scene, visual reminders of the soldiers' cartographic function are always present, playing complex roles. Jimmy, for example, extends the students' regular concentration on etymologies to wonder about the etymology of *theodolite*. The word's actual etymology is obscure, though the *Oxford English Dictionary* speculates that it is an "unscholarly formation" from the Greek for "I see." Jimmy, however, links *theodolite* to "*Theo—theos*—something to do with a god. Maybe *thea*—a goddess!" Typically, Jimmy moves quickly from the divine to the bawdily human: "What shape's the yoke?" (11). Doalty, who has stolen the theodolite as part of his "statement" of opposition to the British surveyors, also finds in it an opportunity for the bawdy, grabbing Bridget around the waist and inquiring "What d'you make of that for an implement, Bridget? Wouldn't that make a great aul shaft for your churn?" (12). The characters' ability to find in a cold scientific instrument metaphors for the divine and the sexual is a reminder of life's complications and of the different ways of knowing. It also hints at the presumption of cartographers, who assume a godlike ability to comprehend and control space.

The blank map dominant in Acts Two and Three is an even more powerful reminder that *Translations* is about more than linguistic imperialism. Colonialism is fundamentally a matter of territory, of space. England is consolidating and organizing "its" space, with a clear eye to imposing not only the linguistic unity of a standard language but also unified social and governmental practices. The simultaneous push for national schools that would end the hedge school system and impose English language instruction began with the creation of a National Education Board in 1831 and is part of the same colonial consolidation effort.[35] The unstated assumption that urban spaces will inevitably control rural ones is parallel to the unstated assumption that, in drama, rural characters will not represent serious issues. All maps reveal the purposes of their makers—railroad maps, road maps, subway maps, geological survey maps, navigation maps, MapQuest, or the interactive 3D geospatial maps used by today's militaries and by crews cleaning up oil spills. When the English ordnance crew has finished its mapping, Ballybeg seems unlikely to remain at the center even of Donegal, the position it occupies for residents who know the rest of the world only as it spreads outward from their center. Arguably this will provide a clearer sense of where and how residents belong. But they must now fit into a very different context, so arguably the map will destroy their sense of place and leave them a paper outline that suggests they belong in an area on the fringes of both Ireland and the British Empire.

Mapping allows colonizers to assert financial and military control over colonized territory. Captain Lancey is somewhat clumsily direct about this aspect of his effort, but Owen deliberately obscures such realities when he translates for the colonized inhabitants. The "modern" world exemplified by these English-speaking colonizers is also here associated with the "modern" scientific method of knowing by measuring the surface of the world. The narrative skills of *dinnseanchas* are being replaced by the calculating skills of geometry as ways of understanding the world, and culture is treated as though it were diagramable. Time is giving way to space as a way of understanding the world. This may be an inevitable and even a desirable development, but it is not a neutral one, and it involves a conscious movement away from reliance on the mythical and historical truths represented by the classics and by the history of local place-names. It also leads, probably inevitably, to the sort of subversion and opposition symbolized by Doalty's disruption of the surveyors' measuring, and by Manus's refusal to observe "polite" social norms and speak English.[36] Like the hedge school response to penal laws and like Irish drama's focus on rural, peasant Ireland, these subversive actions reveal the Irish people's tendency to define themselves in opposition. Samuel Beckett perhaps summed the situation up best when, asked if he were English, he replied simply "Au contraire."[37]

Henri Lefebvre began his 1974 study of social space with the assertion that "not so many years ago, the word 'space' had a strictly geometrical meaning: the idea it evoked was simply that of an empty area." Lefebvre went on to describe the impact: "Space came to dominate, by containing them, all senses and all bodies . . . [There was a] shift from the philosophy to the science of space, [and] mathematicians, in the modern sense of the word, emerged as the proprietors of a science . . . quite clearly detached from philosophy—a science which considered itself both necessary and self-sufficient."[38] Lefebvre lays out the challenges resulting from the separation of mathematical space from both mental space and social space and argues for awareness of "social space" as more than geometry. Considered in isolation, he concludes, space is an empty abstraction. Friel's play begins in a world where mental space and social space are close relatives. The introduction of cartography (mathematical space) disrupts Ballybeg's stable notions of space and moves it toward Lefebvre's empty abstraction.

Most twentieth- and twenty-first-century Westerners believe maps are good things. They may be used for unpopular military or colonial purposes, but the graphing of space seems generally a valuable development. *Translations* presents both the shift to English and the shift to mapped space not as developments to be lamented, but rather as developments that indicate profound changes requiring thoughtful consideration and adjustment. Both translation and mapping are instances of seismic social shifts with powerful impacts on ways of understanding places and determining who does or does not belong in those places. Replacing the local language and understandings of space with "modern" (and clearly imperialist) expressions and understandings alienates these residents from their native language and from the places where they have always lived. Still residents who belong, they are now asked to perceive through an alien lens established by outsiders. The scientific survey and the English language are emblems of modernity, not tradition. They make Ireland other to the Irish and seek to bring Irish ways of knowing into conformity with English ways of knowing. Both maps and language raise questions about how people construct meaning; both are lines and letters on paper that suggest that traditional Irish ways of knowing and belonging are lesser and inferior. "A map," suggests Declan Kiberd, "will have much the same relation to a landscape as the written word has to speech. Each is a form of translation." And Kiberd goes on to quote, with approval, Edward Said's conclusion that "it seems a common human failing to prefer the authority of a text to the disorientations of direct encounters with the human."[39]

Maps also represent an early instance of the sort of globalization that Patrick Lonergan's recent study considers in relation to Irish drama.[40] If our own homelands are understood as a two-dimensional chart, can we not understand other homelands in the same way, and thus understand them equally well? Globalization may be a vague term, but the precision of maps suggests firm and scientific understanding.

Lancey, the least sympathetic of the British in the play, is the cartographer. It is possible that his prickliness results not only from his Englishness and his military position but also from the fact that he shares the common understanding that hedge schoolmasters, free of the authority of both priest and king, were likely to be members of (or clear sympathizers with) radical Irish political organizations threatening the empire. Carleton characterizes "most" of the hedge school teachers as "leaders of illegal associations."[41] Lancey's stiffness is part of his resistance to that potential threat, and he finishes his work efficiently. He struggles, though, to describe the process in ways he believes the locals will understand: "A map is a representation on paper—a picture—you understand picture?—a paper picture—showing, representing this country—yes?—showing your country in miniature—a scaled drawing on paper of—of—of—" (33). Friel's parodic rendering of the difficulties involved in speaking through a translator to people you believe are less intelligent and sophisticated than you are is a funny dramatic set piece that delights audiences.[42] Lancey, however, is not inarticulate. When he wisely follows Owen's advice to "*assume* they understand" and leave the translating to Owen, Lancey provides a fluid explanation entirely reliant on the scientific language with which he is comfortable: "His Majesty's government has ordered the first ever comprehensive survey of this entire country—a general triangulation which will embrace detailed hydrographic and topographic information and which will be executed to a scale of six inches to the English mile" (33). Lancey goes on to read "two brief extracts from the white paper which is our governing charter." The bulk of those "extracts" are direct quotes from the 1824 Spring Rice Report that led to the historical Ordnance Survey.[43] Lancey's original stuttered "of—of—of," however, signals the difficulty of summing up precisely what it is that a map does. The inarticulate *of*s are finally more profound and thought-provoking than the subsequent smooth assemblage of technolanguage focused on hydrographic and topographic information.

Owen's translation of Lancey's remarks is not exactly literal. Hugh and Manus understand English, and Manus later criticizes his brother for mistranslating. It is hard, though, to escape the sense that a "correct" translation of Lancey's explanation would have been challenging: did nineteenth-century Irish (lacking even a word for *map*) have words for *triangulation, hydrographic, topographic*? Would the concept *executed to a scale of six inches to the English mile* have made sense to the residents of Ballybeg? The change that is taking place is not only linguistic. It is also a change in ways of knowing a territory. And arguably the mapping gaze is more typical of the "masculine" colonizer than of the "feminine" colonized. To the colonizer, unmapped space is likely to seem dangerous and unruly. Triangulation is a more valuable mode of understanding than the eyes and memories of the inhabitants. In the 1970s, when Friel was writing, Irish postcolonialists and poststructuralists frequently discussed the need to balance colonialists' understandings with postcolonial understandings—to review territory abandoned by colonial powers and fill in not the white spaces on a surface map of territory but the white spaces in cultural understanding.[44] That discussion underlies the debate embodied in this play.

Yolland, a considerably more sympathetic British soldier, is not a cartographer but an orthographer. His responsibility is not scientific measurement and two-dimensional drawing of space, but naming, which Owen describes as an effort "to denominate and at the same time describe" (40) an area. Denomination and description must go hand in hand, because landscape and language are paired. Yolland has difficulty abandoning traditional Irish place-names, even when they do not seem to make sense, partly because he has a falsely romantic view of Ireland, but also because he has been less completely converted to scientific means of knowing space. His flashes of articulateness come not when he reverts to scientific language but when he speaks of the knowledge of his heart.

If various ways of understanding the space outside the hedge school window are embodied in the language the characters speak, they are most clearly signaled by the map that dominates the stage space.[45] In the school interior, human beings cluster around an abstract representation of the space outside—a representation that does not include people and thus suggests that the world may be adequately described by a grid of surface lines and symbols. Ballybeg is represented on the Ordnance Survey map from a perspective the residents themselves can share only imaginatively. To survey is literally *to oversee*. The English word *oversee* also means to manage an estate or colony. A map "sees" the landscape from above, a perspective unavailable to these Donegalers (or to any humans before the advent of airplanes and satellites). Residents, however, see it more immediately and see the surface less expansively, more narrowly yet also more deeply. Part of what the Irish characters are resisting is the suggestion that the map's expansive surface gaze (its survey) represents an adequate way of knowing their world. The tension between that surface view and their own historical or cultural view is inescapable.

The Irish know their literal place very differently than the map does, and they understand their figurative place very differently than the English do. Doalty, convinced the English will clear the countryside in response to Yolland's disappearance, observes, "*(simply, altogether without irony)* And after all the trouble you went to, mapping the place and thinking up new names for it" (83).

Garrett Sullivan has pointed out that King Lear's map indicates the division of his kingdom into three, and that the three political kingdoms "evoke" England, Scotland, and Wales. In *Translations*, the map represents not a movement to divide a kingdom but a movement to unite Ireland more closely to the rest of Great Britain. Both maps, though, are efforts to achieve political boundaries by what Sullivan calls "monarchical fiat, with no attention paid to the people affected."[46] Terence Hawkes describes *King Lear* as a text that "interogat[es] King James' efforts to present the throne as the source and guarantee of social coherence."[47] *Translations* functions in a somewhat parallel way, interrogating the nineteenth-century Ordnance Survey effort to produce social coherence. Because no king (or prime minister or other governmental figure) is mentioned, responsibility for the assumption that governmental fiat can achieve political unity rests generally with the British government. In an area as obsessed with the drawing or erasing of borders as both Irelands have been for decades, the implications of the map and mapping extend well beyond the historical period during which the play is set. However involved we become with *Translations* as a love story, as a tale of linguistic imperialism, as a picture of education, or as a story of father and sons, the stage space provides a constant reminder that this is also a play about the spaces of Ireland—how they are known, how they are described, how they are controlled, who belongs in them and who does not.

A fundamental irony in Friel's dramatic consideration of space is that Ballybeg is not a real place, but an imagined one. His imagined small town, the setting for most of his plays, belongs to the real County Donegal, yet the town itself is no less artificial than the geometric plotting of the Ordnance Survey map. Fictional town and scientific map are alternative, incompatible ways of understanding "reality," and the tension between them cannot be erased. Like many things in this play—and elsewhere in Friel's body of work—the presentation is not rhetorical but dialectical. Friel asks not that we dismiss any of the alternatives (cartography or *dinnseanchas*, geography or narrative, mathematics or myth), but that we consider what we learn from each, and that we recognize the inevitability of change. *Always* is "not a word [to] start with. It's a silly word" (90).

Hugh's equanimity (at the end of Act Two) in accepting the inevitability of change does not represent an optimistic view of the future, however. It may be possible to view Maire's promised departure as a sign of hope (like Nora's departure in *A Doll's House*), but Manus's departure (unlike Christy's in *The Playboy of the Western World*) holds little promise. Neither their departures nor Owen's return is a solution. Family and community are shattered. The potato crop will fail. The fatherless baby born in Act One is buried in Act Three. Balleybeg nurtures neither children nor crops. Like the places of other plays examined in this study, Balleybeg is a place where traditional nuclear families no longer exist, and where future generations do not survive, let alone thrive. If plot details alone leave the possibility that this portion of Ireland will survive in anything like the form that these nineteenth-century inhabitants know it, the play's conjunction of language and interior space with the external world reminds us of what we already know: that the changes are irreversible. The maps being made represent a way of understanding space familiar to contemporary audiences. And the battle to stave off cultural change by preserving the Irish language has been lost so completely that Friel (knowing he cannot count on audiences to understand Irish) has his characters speaking English even when audiences are to presume they are speaking Irish. Though it remains part of Irish cultural memory, the Balleybeg of *Translations* no longer exists. It is home to no one. And no one belongs there, however much we wish it were otherwise.

CHAPTER 2

Picturing a Changing Landscape

Conor McPherson's *The Weir* (1997)

> Places as such are dead
> Or nearly
>   —Derek Mahon, "Brighton Beach"

Conor McPherson has given mixed signals about the relationship between his 1997 play *The Weir* and contemporary Ireland. In 1998, for example, he insisted that he "had never set out to write consciously about my country" and backed away from suggestions that the play is "concerned with geography or politics. I am from the Republic of Ireland and that's where my plays have their genesis, but not from any need to address anything about my country."[1] A year later, recalling the play's origins, McPherson emphasized a somewhat different point: "I had some pangs of guilt and remorse. What gave me the right to situate a piece of fiction so firmly in a real place?"[2] The text of the play specifies a setting in "a rural part of Ireland, Northwest Leitrim or Sligo,"[3] but programs for both the 1998 and the 2008 productions at the Gate Theatre specify merely "a remote part of Ireland," as though to head off any overly specific identification of the play's territory, and dialogue makes no mention of the particular portion of Ireland that is home for these characters.

McPherson's desire to forestall relegation of his work to some narrowly "Irish" category is understandable, particularly since his denial of geographic or political concerns came as part of his insistence that, like other residents of the Republic, he was removed from issues swirling around the North's Troubles—issues that were animating numerous other late twentieth-century Irish plays. On the other hand, *The Weir*'s setting *is* recognizably Irish, and McPherson took the director and set designer of the opening production to Leitrim so they could get a feel for the area's pubs and landscape, including the Electricity Supply Board (ESB) dam on the River Shannon from which the play takes its title.[4] McPherson's indication that the production of this play, which takes place entirely indoors, needed to arise from a clear sense of the landscape and the weir confirms the complex relationship between the interior space of the set and the exterior space around which so much dialogue circles. The play may be set in an interior, but it is by understanding exterior space that characters establish their status as among those who belong.

When the curtain goes up on *The Weir*, evocations of formulaic Irish drama are easy to find. Regulars in McPherson's bar have gathered around the fire in early spring—part of the traditional harvest-to-planting storytelling season. Aging photos are mounted on the wall. The bar's patrons are male; the fire is peat; the preferred drink is Guinness. Stage directions specify that "this bar is part of a house and the house is part of a farm" (3), almost a truncated version of the progression in *A Portrait of the Artist as a Young Man*, in which Stephen situates himself step-by-step in class, college, county, country, continent, world, and universe. The bar is simultaneously separate from and part of the surrounding geography that regularly intrudes on the dialogue of the patrons. It is literally home for Brendan, the owner-bartender, and metaphorically home for two other aging bachelors, long-term residents who belong there as others do not and who converse in the shorthand of bar habitués comfortable with each other but unaccustomed to articulate self-revelation. Audiences are likely to think they know precisely where they are. Like tourists who respond to promotional brochures and head for Donegal, audiences have arrived in the theater to observe an isolated and therefore unique place. Like tourists, the largely urban audiences are consuming a more rural space and satisfying an appetite for difference and novelty, entering (however briefly) a world that is not their own.

The Weir fits neither into the familiar genre of Irish nationalist plays with which the Abbey Theatre began[5] nor into the familiar genre of Troubles plays. And it is not, as one reviewer labeled it, "A requiem for Ireland."[6] Nor is it, as other reviews indicated, set in an Irish pub where "time stands still," demonstrating that "old Ireland is possessed by its past" (a particularly puzzling judgment, since the play's characters have difficulty remembering Ireland's past). The play is, however, Irish in more than its genesis, and McPherson's handling of space occasionally seems an illustration for textbook analysis of Irish cultural and theatrical traditions, and of the ways those traditions manipulate space. The play's broad appeal throughout the English-speaking world, though, indicates that its use of both theatrical and geographic space, including awareness of space in the contemporary commercial world, resonates with non-Irish viewers as well.

The English-speaking world is familiar with key elements of the easily commodified romantic pastoral tradition associated with rural Ireland, the western portion of which artist Paul Henry (1876–1958) famously termed "the very soul of Ireland."[7] Even today, descriptions on tourist websites laud the breathtaking, "charming . . . dramatic scenery"; the "delightful green glens" of Leitrim; gothic and prehistoric ruins that loose the imagination.[8] Pubs (the "warmest places on earth," according to *Discover Ireland*) will be venues for magical storytelling. Leitrim is different than urban, culturally polyglot Dublin, and fairies still come down from the hills.[9] The appeal of this romantic tradition is evident in the program and posters for the 1998 Gate Theatre production of *The Weir*, which presented not the interior of the bar, but a photographic view of a mountain stream with what seems to be a cottage in the background. The fact that the photo also includes what might be a weir and what are certainly dimly seen power lines adds complexities, but the dominant image is that of a mystical rural landscape—an indication that the theater's marketers anticipated the appeal of this pastoral view for the urban audiences they hoped to attract. Publicity for McPherson's play, then, no less than the tourist brochures that have brought tourists to rural Ireland, provided a "commodified and marketable" version of Ireland that is not rooted in contemporary reality.[10]

By contrast, descriptions of both the stage space and the surrounding geographic space reveal an area quite unlike de Valera's famous 1940s romantic evocation of a self-sufficient rural Ireland, with maidens dancing at crossroads. The single set represents the constricted interior of the bar, whose geographic surroundings regularly intrude on the dialogue of patrons. Though reviews, and often McPherson himself in interviews, refer to the set as a "pub," the stage directions specify not "pub" but "bar." That change in nomenclature is one indication of the extent to which the Ireland of Synge and Yeats has been wired into the modern era, no longer immune from external, even international, influences.[11] This bar has an old television and a radio (neither turned on) and a stove built into the fireplace. The fuel is not hand-cut turf but machine-cut briquettes. One character needs spectacles; another wears "slip-on shoes" (3). The bar serves not only Guinness and Harp, but also brandy and even wine. There is a loo, albeit an out-of-order one. Earlier Irish stage pubs, like 1950s U.S. television drama, were careful not to mention toilet facilities (whether indoor or outdoor) or the need to use them. Patrick Duffy points out that the Rural Electrification Scheme of which the Shannon's weir was a part resulted in a "rash of bathroom extensions" in rural Ireland.[12] Patrons of this bar are beneficiaries.

Evidences of a changed environment are everywhere in the dialogue, as well as on the set. We learn that additions have been made to both house and bar. The new road bypasses and isolates Jack's garage, reducing his business. Residents have moved on to Carrick or Dublin or the United States, and tourists have arrived. McPherson, born just two years before Ireland entered the European Union, is portraying a less-isolated rural Ireland than had earlier dramatists, noting changes in transportation and communication that have shrunk the world and altered understandings of space. The specification that the television is old and that neither television nor radio is turned on may indicate that residents are reluctant to allow the changing outside world to intrude on the world where they belong. They cannot completely avoid the arrival of outsiders, however, and the deliberate inclusion of late twentieth-century details emphasizes the area's movement toward urbanization and globalization.

Black-and-white photographs on the wall are clear indications that the past persists in this contemporary establishment. They show a ruined abbey, the Electricity Supply Board weir, and a town in a cove among mountains. Audiences, of course, even in a small venue, would have difficulty identifying the photos, but they are the excuse for considerable commentary as the men seek to inform Valerie about her new home, insisting that the photos are no more "fake" than the history they narrate. For anyone anticipating a stereotypical portrait of rural Ireland, the conversation about the photos is surprising, revealing an Irish world that has moved past its past. For these contemporary Irish men, the very outlines of that past are fuzzy, and they no longer view the land as practical pasture, finding it instead a site of beauty, or simply space to be marketed. Nevertheless, their desire to make Valerie feel at home takes the form of introducing her to the area's long human history.

Neither stage directions nor dialogue indicates that this bar has a window, so exterior space enters not when characters look out a window and describe what they see (as characters in *Translations* and *The Playboy of the Western World* do), but rather when they look at photographs and describe what they see. The impact of the photographs deserves consideration in light of what Susan Sontag has observed about the complex impact of photography in general, which "has become one of the principal devices for experiencing something, for giving an appearance of participation."[13] Sontag's point about photographs parallels the impact of René Magritte's 1933 painting *La Condition Humaine*, in which a landscape painting, mounted on an easel before a window, becomes indistinguishable from the view it depicts. "What lies beyond the windowpane of our apprehension, says Magritte, needs a design before we can properly discern its form, let alone derive pleasure from its perception."[14] In *The Weir*, everything that characters mention about the surrounding landscape is filtered through images in the photographs, and everything audiences learn is filtered first through the photographs and then through the characters' stories. This constitutes not so much participation itself as the appearance of participation.[15] Photography is closely linked with the middle-class status of the never-seen-but-often-discussed tourists who come to McPherson's bar. Like the weir, the photographs are instances of industrialization, indications that Ireland is participating in modernity even as it markets tradition. The Chinese boxes framing the perceptions of audiences sitting in a darkened theater watching characters on stage discuss photographs, are multiple and complex, a fact to which McPherson pointed in the Author's Note discussing his plays in a 1996 collection: "These plays are set 'in a theatre.' Why mess about? The character is *on stage*, perfectly aware that he is talking to a group of people."[16] Alone among the plays considered in this study, *The Weir* suggests an awareness that landscape is neither untouched environmental space nor merely practical space for human activity. Instead, the play presents landscape as an environment that has been changed by human activity, and characters show some awareness that the history of their homeland should include awareness of what humans have altered its landscape and how they have altered it.

The presence of a television and a radio, though they remain dark and silent, suggests the potential that technology will eventually disrupt and displace not only the photographs but also the stories the bar patrons tell each other. The fact that Brendan has photographs on the wall suggests a lingering nostalgia. The fact he has not turned on the television or radio suggests a continued preference for storytelling. If the entertainment technologies were used, there would be no play, of course. Their existence on stage is a reminder that once the technology is switched on patrons will focus on it, rather than interacting through storytelling. Audiences would then have no reason even to be in the theater. Meanwhile, in the liminal world of Brendan's bar, a mixture of traditional and transformational, patrons both venture into the past and connect with the future.

The landscape photograph on the wall is the view from the field above the bar, where Brendan does not pasture sheep because it is "Too much trouble driving a herd up" (4). His sisters, who live elsewhere, want him to sell the field so that, he says, they can buy "new cars for the hubbies" (4). The self-sufficient, one-hearth peasant farm is nowhere in sight, and these are not the stereotypical Celts whose image Seamus Deane has described as "dreamy, imaginative, indifferent to the material world."[17] These residents of rural Ireland are increasingly mobile and practical. Brendan may not share his sisters' bottom-line orientation, resisting both the notion that he could rent space in the field as tourist campsites and his sisters' desire to sell the field. In part, he resists because of the fairy road that runs through the field, yet his resistance relies on something—presumably his bar and its tourist patronage—to supply alternate income. Finbar patronizingly suggests that Brendan must not see "too many" of the pre-euro twenty-pound notes (17), but Brendan is clearly surviving and able to stand him to a round or two. His sisters see the field through the "rational" lens of real estate capitalism and regard land as a salable commodity. He sees the field through the "rational" lens of capitalistic tourism and regards landscape as a visual commodity that may be sold to tourists. Both attitudes represent shifts in traditional rural understandings of space. When the field was a pasture, it was economically important to the owners who drove their herds to it. That economic importance was intimate and personal, very different than the economic importance of land to commercial farmers who hire wage-earning workers to produce commodities that may be marketed to distant consumers. Brendan and his sisters represent neither of these agricultural relationships with the field, but their approaches to it do not lack economic concerns. Unlike Bull McCabe in John B. Keane's *The Field* (1965) and Xavier Cassidy in *By the Bog of Cats . . .* , Brendan has no desire to put his land to agricultural use. He is also unlike William Dee in *The Field*, who wishes to put land to industrial use, and unlike Hester Swane in *By the Bog of Cats . . .* , who not only wants to leave the space of the bog alone but also spends time in it. *The Weir*, though, presents a similarly multidimensional rural world in which the forces of pastoralism and consumer tourism meet and redefine the place where these characters feel at home.

None of these economic factors is new in Ireland, where issues of land ownership (and the profits arising from it) have long been inseparable from politics, and where travel literature from the nineteenth century on has focused on rural-urban contrasts between Ireland and England. A well-established early and ongoing purpose of such writing was to domesticate the impoverished Irish landscape for an audience of more-affluent tourists, who would then be encouraged to visit.[18]

Another picture on the wall is of the weir itself, an Electricity Supply Board dam built on the River Shannon as part of the Rural Electrification Scheme that began at the end of the 1940s. The bar's regular patrons finally agree that the photo, in which their fathers appear, was taken in 1951, but they show little awareness of what the dam means. They know, of course, that before the dam there was no electricity in the area, and many of the ghostly stories they tell are atmosphered by darkness. But it was their fathers who witnessed electrification's transformation of the area. Rivers are as tightly linked to Irish national identity as is the rural landscape, appearing as personified keystone representations on Dublin's Customs House, and even represented on the backs of some pre-euro Irish banknotes, so the photograph of the weir, which irrevocably changed the Shannon's flow, has implications for the impact of industrialization on Ireland's national identity.

It is arguable, of course, that the weir or, for that matter, the pier in Brian Friel's *Wonderful Tennessee*, which represents a similar industrial modification of the landscape, could be removed so that the area would return to preindustrial status. Removal is unlikely. Furthermore, removal of the structures would not remove their impact: the shape of river and sea shore have been altered by dam and pier; patterns of erosion have changed; the contours of the land have shifted in ways as radical as the shifts of occupation and lifestyle.

As described by McPherson's characters, the photograph of the weir warrants comparison to *Night's Candles Are Burnt Out* (1928), by Sean Keating, who had been "commissioned by the Electricity Supply Board to execute a series of pictures recording the development of the hydro-electric scheme on the river Shannon."[19] Keating's painting has been called "an allegory on the new Ireland of the Free State" in which "national identity is incorporated into the painting's theme of progress."[20] Both widespread romanticism about rural Ireland and celebrations of Irish progress are contexts for McPherson's play, which shares with them a concern for Irish national identity but presents what, to a contemporary eye, seems a more-nuanced reality than either of those more-simplistic earlier allegories.

Fáilte Ireland and The Heritage Council have been more self-conscious than Brendan about the tight link between cultural and natural heritage and the tourist industry that is important to Ireland's economy. Their 2009 joint publication "Climate Change, Heritage and Tourism" describes precisely the connections between space, heritage, and economy revealed in Brendan's bar. It also emphasizes the importance of preserving the island's industrial heritage and notes that the Heritage Act of 1995 "made provision . . . for the designation of structures in public ownership . . . [such as] the Electricity Supply Board, as heritage buildings."[21] Work by both government and private organizations in Ireland indicates a strong and increasing awareness that industrialization is as important as older indications of human impact on the landscape—Ireland is a place of modernism as well as traditionalism. McPherson's characters have a contemporary, if vague, awareness of this mix of factors, though they continue to shape their understandings through the traditional art of storytelling, an art that John Cashman argues persists in Ireland and often involves just the sort of stories these characters tell: humorous local character anecdotes, brief biographical narratives, memories.[22] The cosmopolitan influences of the European Union, global communication, and travel have not completely displaced insularity and traditional patterns of belief and behavior. Still, the play's focus on the construction of houses, roads, and weir represents an awareness of landscape as modified by human construction. It is not only the history of people in a place but also the history of people in a place they have physically modified that constitutes homeland.

Local understanding of more-distant, preindustrial times is even fuzzier than is awareness of the weir's history, despite the fact that the area retains the tangible artifacts of history. No one is precisely sure when the abbey was less than a ruin, but they are all clear it was once important, even if they struggle to interpret the remains. "This was like the capital of the, the county, it would have been" (19), Jim explains. His uncertainty about traditional units of space like "county" highlights changes that have removed such spatial designations from the list of things residents regard as important about their homeland. The ruined landscape continues, in J. W. Foster's words, to "[bear] witness to a dignified preconquest culture," and he suggests the details of the landscape need "to be read like manuscripts as well as to be appreciated like paintings."[23] Landscape in this play, however, seems more accurately described in John Montague's terms: a "manuscript" the residents have lost the ability to read.[24] Similar landscapes have provided picturesque subject matter for painters who often do not include any of the presumably less picturesque humans, and they allow sentimental tourists a temporary respite from the present.[25] These bar patrons, however, are not particularly nostalgic about their homeland's past. For them, the ruins serve no purpose, and their interest in the past is as vague as their knowledge of the tourists' nationality. Lacking a local heritage center, even residents struggle to imagine what their homeland was for earlier inhabitants.

The play's language is a key indicator that this is not Synge's western world. McPherson has repeatedly cited David Mamet as an important early influence,[26] and this play's dialogue reveals much of that influence. While not quite Mametspeak, McPherson's language nevertheless shares important characteristics with that of his American model: it is sparse and dully repetitious vernacular, cliché-ridden and studded with ellipses and the f-word.[27] Even when characters are narrating tales they have clearly told before, McPhersonspeak is not the lyrical Irish-English, spiced with Gaelic constructions and exclamations, stereotypically associated with the green glens and romantic ruins beloved by tourists. Nor is it the challenging dialect of *By the Bog of Cats* . . . . When a woman enters the male enclave of this bar, the patrons seek to charm her with what might pass for Irishness, but for the most part McPherson's characters support Yeats' romantic belief that "the mass of the people cease to understand any poetry when they cease to understand the Irish language, which is the language of their imaginations."[28] The rhythm and vocabulary of the dialogue signal that rural Ireland has changed.

The photographs on the bar's wall illustrate this changing world, which is pictured at various points in time. The stories that characters tell and Valerie's hope that the area will provide a new home, a site of renewal for her, make it clear that rural Ireland, like Wordsworth's Tintern Abbey, is part of the "mighty world" that eye and ear both "perceive" and "half create."[29]

Often the play's title is taken as a metaphor for the dammed-up feelings that will spill out in stories, and McPherson has endorsed that understanding: "On one side [it] is quite calm, and on the other side water is being squeezed through. Metaphorically, the play is about a breakthrough. Lots under the surface is coming out."[30] Ian Rickson, who directed the premiere, shared the understanding that the dam was a metaphor for the flood of feeling released.[31] Nicholas Grene echoes both playwright and director in describing the weir as "a metaphor for the controlled release of emotion through talk and storytelling," and concludes that the weir is not "a symbol of a stage in the modernization of Ireland."[32] The weir *does* serve as a metaphor for dammed-up emotion, and McPherson's bar is not simply a synecdoche for Ireland—certainly not for the Celtic Tiger so powerful in early twenty-first century thinking about the island. But modernization *is* an issue. The bar continues the familiar Irish dramatic trope of home as metaphor for nation, and characters whose ages range from thirties to fifties (all of them older than McPherson was when he wrote the play) represent the sweep of time. Both stage directions and dialogue refer to the weir as an ESB weir, and the impact of electricity is evident throughout.

A surveyor's platting of land so that it becomes a marketable commodity may be seen as what Matthew Johnson terms a "reappropriation of old familiar things in a new way . . . even as their shape remains the same."[33] The weir, by contrast, actually changes the pattern of material space and involves what Johnson terms a "cultural redefinition" of space.[34] It is also one of many forces in the play that contribute to what Patrick Duffy has described in another context as "a form of landscape trauma" that has "irreversibly altered" the material and emotional heritage of Ireland.[35] The play illustrates the distinction between seeing landscape as "a space or collection of spaces" and seeing it as "the setting of certain human activities."[36]

The content of the photos, the presence of toilets and wine, and the surprising occupations of the bar patrons emerge only gradually, a pacing important to the play's use of and presentation of space. It is often noted that McPherson begins his plays in a naturalistic world and then gradually introduces the supernatural, ghostly elements so crucial to his drama, moving deliberately from naturalism to a more complex reality. The same gradual movement is evident in his handling of setting. The curtain rises on a world seemingly familiar from previous Irish plays, and the entrance of two aging-bachelor bar regulars seems to confirm that this is a familiar dramatic space. The language may lack lyricism, but conversation is easy, familiar, habitual. The plot device that will animate this closed world is also conventional—the introduction of a stranger, an outsider in the bar and in the area. The ease with which this stranger enters the conversation and camaraderie typifies another characteristic of the bar. Like many such establishments, it is a place where strangers may quickly establish a sense of belonging and speak freely. In *The Weir* the footloose, mobile, exciting stranger is not a man, but a woman. When sexual tensions begin to shape the dialogue and subsequent storytelling, then, they are sexual tensions that reverse the gender relations of Synge's *Playboy*: in *The Weir* it is men who seek to garner favor with a woman, and this woman is independent enough (both financially and psychologically) not to show much sexual interest in any of these boyos, and to narrate a story of her own that trumps the male storytelling begun, at least in part, to intrigue and perhaps to intimidate her. Step by step, then, McPherson's play introduces an Irish world different than the romantic world of nineteenth-century Abbey Theatre peasant drama.

In this play, McPherson's only drama with a rural setting, Ireland remains a place of green fields, local shops, and family businesses that have not yet been crowded out by retail chains. The setting echoes details from an experience he has repeatedly cited as one inspiration: boyhood visits from his North Dublin home to his widowed grandfather in Leitrim. "The loneliness struck me ... I'm getting away with an image of Ireland in which Dublin is very far away."[37] The isolated locale constitutes for characters as well as audiences a counterpoint to contemporary urban realities, a place where urbanites might be able to leave behind the pressures of modernity and lapse into an older way of life minimally contaminated by dehumanizing industrialization. The typically urban audiences are likely to share with Valerie (and with the characters in Friel's *Wonderful Tennessee*) a desire to escape their urban homes for a rural isolation where they imagine they might belong to a world still friendly to the supernatural. "The play is about breaking [from] the ordinary world and allowing the supernatural to flow in, and finding out what your fears are" the playwright says.[38]

The rural landscape photo on the 1998 Gate Theatre program seems designed to appeal both to Irish audiences and to audiences at the Royal Court Theatre in London, where the production premiered. The cover of the 1998 Royal Court text has a close-up of a man holding a glass of Guinness in which a small child is either swimming or drowning. Ten years later, the program for a Gate Theatre production directed by Garry Hynes displayed a cover photograph of individuals clustered closely against a blank interior wall and clad in ways suggestive of the early twentieth century. Their images are blurred and puzzling. McPherson's 2008 program note, titled "Old Haunts," begins with the story of his encounter with the Gate Theatre ghost. That same program has a centerfold that is haunting in a different way: dark branches of bare winter trees silhouetted against a misty sky in which hovers a flock of birds. Juxtaposing such varied images is a reminder of the complexity of this seemingly simple play, which is about all the things suggested in these program images—and more.

McPherson's rural world has moved far beyond little rural shebeens, and the transformations are everywhere evident. These male bar patrons, most of them stereotypically single, spend their nondrinking time selling real estate, preparing sauces for restaurant cuisine, and fixing cars and tractors. They may be rural, but they are not peasant. Brendan is waiting for the lucrative influx of "German" tourists, who may, in reality, be either Danish or Norwegian. Everyone knows the tourists do not belong in this area, but no one is sure (or much cares) where they *do* belong. The tourists will arrive and spend money, but they will not notice "the shadow from the Knock moving along the floor, with the sun going down" (49) because they are too busy "playing all old sixties songs on their guitars. And they don't even know the words" (49). Despite the presence of some crusty old bachelors who are fond of a pint, this is not the world of Synge's *Playboy*, but a consumer democracy with multinational influences. Brendan wants to preserve the fairy ring at the top of the field for other reasons, but he also knows that the picturesqueness of the landscape and culture is part of what has been marketed to tourists. In an increasingly familiar irony, the presence of tourists threatens the very picturesqueness that brought them. The multinationals sing songs that belong to the locals in the sense that the lyrics seem to be in English, but these are not traditional Irish tunes. Neither the locals nor the tourists appear to care that this bar has no fiddle in the wings.

Tourist promotional literature shares with travelogues an approach dependent on establishing a contrast (often a tension) between home and away, between the familiar and the foreign. That, presumably, is the appeal that has brought tourists to this remote area. Though the tourists are not physically present in the stage space, their annual arrival has required the natives to step out of their usual lives sufficiently to begin to see their own world through foreign eyes, to recognize the strangeness of familiar space. They may understand no more of the Germans than the Germans do of them, but their role as observed other requires a different awareness of the place where they live, and of their place in that place. Arguably, tourism, like mapping, often "affirm[s] the values of the centre, under the guise of taking a 'genuine' . . . interest" in difference.[39] Both geographers and tourists are prone to an unconscious implication that territory does not exist until discovered by the cartographer's sextant or the tourist's viewfinder. This dynamic is heightened when Valerie arrives and the locals quite specifically begin to contemplate the impression they and their world are making on her.

Valerie's presence in the space of the bar is analogous to the audience's presence in the space of the theater. Audiences, like Valerie herself, are privileged observers of a world to which they do not belong, intruders in a space that the play presents as home to these Irish men. The constricted space of the bar in which the "action" takes place emphasizes the closed nature of the characters' world and the intrusiveness of Valerie's presence and the audience's. Audiences, sitting in quiet immobility, are not excluded from the intimate space where characters are almost equally quiet and immobile. The play is generally performed in real time, with no intermission. Characters speak to each other, never breaking the fourth wall, though the playwright has expressed a preference for open sets of the sort Rae Smith designed for *The Weir*. Renovations to the Royal Court Theatre (which had commissioned the play) meant that the premiere took place in a "cordoned-off stage area of the Ambassadors Theatre" with seating for only about sixty. The audience was "pretty much in the bar with the characters."[40] Discussing Smith's set for *The Seafarer*, McPherson noted his hatred of "sets that have walls . . . [an open set] allows more for a possibility of darkness and intimacy and . . . the sense of infinity."[41]

McPherson's paradoxical coupling of "intimacy" and "infinity" captures the world of this play. In a tight interior, characters discuss exterior space and the spirits that animate the material world. Audiences resemble Valerie in their outsider status, but they resemble Brendan in their status as nonnarrating listeners.[42] They share in this confined world because it reaches out to include them. Regardless of how the set is designed, the play highlights the duality of inside and outside as both physical and psychological categories. Interior space is space set aside, divided from the exterior space around which so much of the dialogue revolves. On its simplest level, the interior space of this bar has been set aside for drinking, for protection from the elements, for comradeship. As the evening progresses, though, it becomes clear that the bar is also set-aside space where comradeship can be extended to an outsider who arrives with few interests shared by the locals, except for "the powerful need people have for community."[43]

Like the interior space of *Translations*, the bar offers the possibility of communication. The bar is a space where the imminence of the supernatural can be acknowledged and where human empathy can produce little (and, yes, temporary) miracles of understanding and compassion. Fairies may roam outside. Spirits may enter on the phone line. But it is inside, gathered around the hearth, that human characters and audiences come together. Momentarily, everyone belongs. The immobility of characters on stage is matched by the stillness of audience members in their seats, and both sides of the footlights are linked in listening. "I love it when somebody sits and tells me story after story. That's my favorite kind of companionship," McPherson has said.[44]

While it may be possible to view this bar as purgatorial space where individuals may tell the truth because no one will return, it more closely resembles a sort of sacred space, approximating a church in its ability to bring strangers together in shared communion. Because the audience is included in this communion, the play echoes functions descended from Western drama's origins as religious ritual. Like a church, the bar is public space where highly private concerns may be addressed. In *The Weir* these concerns are not precisely religious, in the narrow sense of that term, but they are spiritual. A haunting question lingers: why does this communion take place in a bar rather than in a church? This is not, of course, a new question, but it helps to define the world of the play, in which it is the ritual of storytelling, not any ritual of prayer or quiet contemplation, that provides solace. The bar's sacred space is simultaneously a theatrical space, where characters act out the versions of themselves that they hope others will perceive. The men are clearly and self-consciously presenting personas they hope will appeal to Valerie, and she is doing the same in relation to them: it is her ability to deliver a narrative as powerful as any of theirs that creates a place for her in an unfamiliar space. Such theatrical rituals of transformation are analogous to those associated with religion: both involve a convergence of the transcendent and the mundane. At the end of the play, everyone (including the audience) leaves this shared theatrical and communal space. No two individuals are headed for the same "home." The characters leave to return to solitary lives in "the real world." The plot device that requires the departure of even Brendan (for whom the bar is literally home) allows the curtain to fall, as it rose, on empty space, providing a visual reminder of the temporary nature of the communion on which the play has focused.

In the cliché drama of rural Ireland, people must move on to find greater opportunity.[45] Often, they move on to the city. In this play, Jack reveals that his first and only love did just that, in the 1960s. Brendan's sisters and their husbands have also left the area, and are willing to sell their bit of rural space to buy cars and gain yet more mobility. Finbar, the character with the most noticeably Irish name, leaves for the slightly more urban nearby Carrick, where he can sell real estate and prepare sauces for his restaurant. The most "modern" and upwardly mobile character, he is also the least likable. Valerie, the newcomer whose name begins with a letter not even found in the Irish alphabet, has reversed this pattern of movement. A young Dublin professional with a job at Dublin City University and a husband on the faculty, she moves to this rural area of lonely bachelors and nonworking bathrooms to heal. Her movement parallels the pattern of McPherson's own engagement with Leitrim. The other characters, though, represent those who have stayed in the place that is their home, whatever its modern difficulties.

Valerie has apparently come to stay, but for the moment her presence resembles that of a tourist. Gerry Smyth, discussing space and the Irish cultural imagination and building on the work of previous commentators, notes that rural Ireland has been marketed as more "authentic": urban tourists can simultaneously feel superior to the "typical" locals and think they have engaged with the authentic.[46] It's no wonder that Jack and Jim decamp to other drinking establishments when the Germans arrive.

Valerie's engagement with the spaces of Ireland raises issues important beyond Ireland. Traditionally, women's mobility has seemed a challenge to a patriarchal society. Escaping the gendered spaces of the domestic and the private—spaces starkly delineated in rural Ireland—women could find employment and freedom in urban areas. Valerie gives no hint that she has ever lived anywhere other than Dublin, but for her the city (a type of social organization created, at least in part, for purposes of defense) has become a place of chaos and pain. Her mobility, an ability to be not only *where* but also *what* she chooses, leads her to a distant, more sheltered place that is also in some ways a place of the past. Valerie is on a quest of sorts, and epic quests across the surface of the earth have typically been male. To use Carol Christ's terms, female quests involve not literal travel, but "diving deep and surfacing."[47] Valerie's arrival in the protected space of the bar is novel not just because she is a female, a traveling female, a female traveling alone. It is novel because she is leaving the East, moving from urban to rural, as had J. M. Synge and Paul Henry.[48] In that movement she is reversing spatial relationships that have dominated the lives of other characters and the development of Irish society.

Asked what identifies his work as "Irish" writing, McPherson replied, "It is the whole notion of Catholicism and the idea of the spiritual world somehow being more real than the material world. Irish people are more concerned about the inner life . . . and the inner response."[49] The ghost stories the bar patrons tell chronicle the changing landscape of these extrarational understandings that McPherson identified as "Irish," but they do not chronicle the power of Catholicism: quite the reverse.

The earliest tale narrates events from 1910, when, Jack says, "there was no electricity out here. And there's no dark like a winter night in the country" (21). The local fairy road was disrupted by construction, and the fairies knocked plaintively on the doors of a house in their path, until a priest was called to bless the doors and the knocking stopped. The fairies returned in the 1950s, when the weir went in. In 1979, when a neighbor girl using a Ouija board is frightened, Finbar's reaction is to call a doctor, not a priest. The young woman's mother phones the priest—a Vatican II priest in whom no one seems to have reposed much confidence. Later, Jack recalls the day a pedophile manifested at his own funeral, in hopes of being buried in the same grave with a young girl, apparently so that he might continue his unsavory behavior after death. The priest's actions at the funeral suggest complicity in covering up the pedophilia. These stories are told, in part, to intrigue and attract Valerie's attention but also because the men are seeking to make her feel at home and because they seek her understanding. In their references to priests—whose role diminishes from ouster of fairies to enabler of pedophiles—the stories make clear that priests are no longer authority figures. There are more sinners than saints in this Ireland. The storytellers, however, show no evidence of being traumatized by a loss of faith. Rather, they satisfy their concern for spirituality by chronicling tales of what seems an older spiritual world, using remnants of that earlier world to create a synthesis of change and continuity. Their homeland is now secular as well as increasingly global. The diminished impact of both fairies and priests is evident. But the inhabitants retain a worldview that is not exclusively literal and nonsacred, and their sense of their home allows for the continued existence of the marvelous, a quality that McPherson has celebrated in numerous interviews and program notes.

Valerie's unflustered acceptance of the men's tales of continued involvement in a spiritual world validates the release of repressed feelings, and the men steadily gain confidence in their narratives. When Valerie herself assumes the mantle of storyteller, she shifts from listener to talker and realigns standard gender relationships. All narratives, of course, are "false" to an extent, because they are shaped versions of unreliable memories. Storytellers assume a pose, and the pose is part of the story. Eamonn Jordan has pointed to intriguing indications that Valerie's story may be more invented than any of the evening's other tales,[50] but regardless of whether audiences—or Valerie, or the listeners in the bar—believe in the accuracy of her tale, Valerie's story shifts the narrative standards established earlier because it is told by a woman who assumes that her power to make meaning matches that of the men.

Because she is a woman, and because she immediately signals her outsider culture by ordering wine, Valerie disrupts a space where generally only these rural men belong. When she herself becomes a narrator, she is empowered through discourse; narrative is no longer produced by those "other" to Valerie, but by Valerie herself, who is "other" to this area and to the gender of the bar's regulars. She is no longer the object of their narratives, but the subject of her own. Because this bar has parallels with a theater, in the sense that each of these characters is performing an identity for the others, it may also be possible to see in Valerie the potential for opening a space for women playwrights in the largely masculine space of Irish drama. That potential remains, however, well in the background, since McPherson is part of the standard male cadre of Irish playwrights.

The spirit of Valerie's accidentally drowned daughter telephones Valerie, in an episode weirdly reminiscent of that odd cult film *Strange Brew* (1983), in which the ghost of Hamlet Senior appears on a video game screen. Valerie's tale implies that the fairies forced from the Irish countryside continue to inhabit the Irish psyche, and that they too have entered the modern technological, urban world. Her story is a counterweight to assertions like Thomas Crofton Croker's nineteenth-century hope that "when rational education shall be diffused among the misguided peasantry of Ireland, the belief in . . . supernatural beings must disappear in that country, as it has done in England, and these 'shadowy tribes' will live only in books."[51] The world of *The Weir* is a world enriched by the refusal of the shadowy tribes to be so easily dismissed.

The complexity of this changing world is indicated by Finbar's description of his cooking as a "superstition" (29) and by discussion of whether Jim's success with the horses is based on a "scientific" approach or "something that's not the facts and figures" (15–16). The authority of doctors and police is no less diminished and suspect than that of priests. Valerie's tale has no priests—only a doctor summoned by her husband to administer calming drugs.[52] Has Valerie's daughter actually called? Has Valerie imagined the call? Does she pretend to find in ancient supernatural beliefs a method of living in the present? Does she really find such a healing synthesis? Answers are unclear. Like rationalist commentators in supernatural stories from "The Fall of the House of Usher" to *The Turn of the Screw*, characters in *The Weir* suggest naturalistic explanations for all the supernatural events—speculating that those who experienced these ghostly presences were victims of practical jokes or distraught or drunk or physically ill or femininely susceptible to impressions. Ultimately, though, the characters accept the emotional realities of the stories, and their sympathetic attendance to those emotional realities bridges the gaps between them.

By the time we reach the present, the storytellers are a long way from fairy roads. Yet the same human development—progress, if you like—that disrupted the fairies also strung the telephone lines that carry Valerie's daughter's call. Whether it is also progress that brings pedophilia is unclear, but it is certainly a contemporary sign that the issue can be discussed in bars and on stage, and that a priest is implicated.

The play's storytelling is a way of shaping and understanding the pain and grief that cross geographical, temporal, and cultural boundaries, a way of reaching out to others. Kristen Morrison has described storytelling in plays by Beckett and Pinter as a "convention for expressing psychological inwardness on stage." Storytelling replaces soliloquy as a "Freudian opportunity to reveal deep and difficult thoughts and feelings while . . . concealing them as fiction or at least distancing them as narration."[53] A comparable inwardness is evident in *The Weir*. As Jack tells it, "learning to listen" (5) once broke his string of bad luck with the horses. More important, for all the characters, learning to listen to others' stories as well as to voice their own is a way to bridge the lonely gulf between individuals and find a space where they may create a temporary family of sorts while their literal families remain either offstage or nonexistent. It is Valerie's husband's inability to listen to what has happened to her that separates her from him emotionally and leads her out of Dublin. And so *The Weir* is a play about the ancient art of storytelling and listening, but it is also a play about contemporary Ireland and about the ongoing value of storytelling in a contemporary world where it might seem to make less sense. The interior space of the bar is a venue in which individuals—individuals who are not drunk—may ease their loneliness by sharing their interior lives. It is also an interior space in which technology, gender relations, and occupations have changed and are changing. Nevertheless, it is a warm, private space in which individuals can and do come together, because of and regardless of exterior realities: a retreat separate from the world of work, a place where drinkers meet with a degree of equality that may not be found outside the bar. If the bar's specialized space allows for a communal gathering, a sort of "found family" reunion, there is no indication that this coming together will persist. When the evening ends, the characters scatter to their individual spaces, which represent the divisions of modern life that can be overcome only temporarily.

Valerie's urban life is apparently deterritorialized, in the sense of being abstracted from a relationship with the spiritual by the influence of capitalism and urbanism. Nature, according to romantic assumptions, is the space in which otherworldly forces continue to move and animate the lives of humans. The city, then, is a space in which the comforts of tradition and ritual are less available. The excitement and freedom of urban life have encouraged the exchange of a sacred world for a secular one. If Valerie arrives at the bar thinking to regain the comfort of a sacralized space that will nurture her spirit, though, she discovers a world in which nature is no longer regarded as imminent with spirit, but as a space to be dammed and controlled, sold to buy cars, marketed to tourists. Even Jim, the forty-year-old bachelor surviving on odd jobs, believes he knows the cash value of his farm (9). For the most part, as the play's interior set emphasizes, these characters are as estranged from the natural world as are their relatives who have moved on. Their dreams of opportunity do not always involve leaving for new homes, but they do involve redefinitions of Irish space from sacred to secular. To use Nicholas Entrikin's terms, this community is shifting from a "subjective" relationship to space in which individuals are "centered" and part of the environment, to an "objective," decentered relationship in which they transcend place. Does place have "inherent value," or do we "assign value" depending on our projects? Does our ability to "control and manipulate" the environment lessen the significance of place? Or does such control alter, without diminishing, the importance of human-environment relations?[54] Place for these characters is less a matter of belonging and more a matter of possessing. Faith in the fairies has been replaced by faith in a mobile, landless future.

Brendan resists selling the top field or renting it as campsites, but his reasons are as much aesthetic as spiritual, and there is no clear sense that he will retain the land for long. In the stories these characters tell each other, though, there remains a sense that the otherworldy may be endangered by "progress" but cannot be defeated. These people erect a bulwark against the uncertainty of the world not so much by resacralizing the world and regaining a traditional sense of cultural identity as by sitting quietly in a confined space and sharing stories. It is the ritual of storytelling rather than the rituals of faeries or priests or doctors that creates a sheltered space, a homelike protection from the dislocations of the world outside. They may have lost the familiar worldview of their ancestors, but their narratives reveal their thinking about—and yearning for—a sacred space. They create that space, and at least a temporary sense of belonging, during an evening of shared fellowship.

That fellowship does not, however, cast a powerful light of hope on the future. These characters have no nurturing families to return to. The only child mentioned has died, and aging bachelors predominate. The field will probably be sold. If the bar survives, it will be only because of the patronage of tourists. (The August 11, 2010, London Daily *Telegraph* noted "The Demise of the Great British Pub," including pictures of a variety of abandoned or ruined establishments throughout the UK. Perhaps pubs are headed for a future parallel to that of the ruins that dot Leitrim.)

The relationship between the confined, intimate space of the bar (the space represented on stage) and the much greater space outside (the space that arrives through narrative and through discussion of the pictures on the wall) is a major shaping factor in the play. The surveyor's plat that divides landscape into marketable lots is as abstract as the cartographic understanding of place evident in *Translations* and indicates not merely a different way of picturing space but a different reason for picturing it. Attempts to preserve spaces and their individual cultures from the impact of commercialism and globalization can include the sort of environmental preservation suggested by Brandon's refusal to sell the upper field. In this play, though, the focus is on preserving local culture by preserving local lore and a narrative, personal sense of space. It is here that the play's focus on storytelling and space come together. The men are telling stories to Valerie, in part, to impress her. They are also telling stories as a way of incorporating her in the place where they live, making her at home in her new home by passing along understandings of the region's history and of its spirit (in all senses of the word). They want her to find a place in their place, and so (like cultural geographers) they share narratives aimed at narrowing the modern gap between place and what place means. Simultaneously, of course, they are reminding themselves of their own places in the region and of their own understanding of its history. Valerie's narrative about the telephone call from her dead daughter suggests that she shares a cultural understanding with them, despite her urban ties and the technological delivery of this message from a spirit. Perhaps she has come precisely because instinct tells her that such communications will not be so readily dismissed in this community.

Events described in McPherson's play span the bulk of the twentieth century (from 1910 to 1997). Characters as well as the setting are often deliberate evocations of clichés—there is a family with 15 children; Jack, a bachelor in his fifties, lives with his mother; Finbar laments the tendency of young women to marry older men; the bar is a comfortable meeting place in a land of fairies; Brendan, the bartender, is the only one who tells no tales, understanding that his almost priestly function (like the function of the bartender in Jim's story) is the healing one of wordless attention. These are both cultural and dramatic clichés, suggesting a rudimentary understanding of Irishness that is as smoothed by reiteration as are the tales told by the characters. McPherson, though, balances them against a most modern world. Michael Billington noted that *The Weir* is replete with "Irish love of fable and a Chekhovian sense of waste."[55] The play is also replete with a Chekhovian sense that times are changing, and even the male drinkers are not entirely opposed to those changes. McPherson, product of an Ireland with an increasingly European focus, is keenly aware of the social complexities that come when women invade men's space, when the imaginations of tourists (or playgoers, or storytellers) transform real places into nostalgic set pieces, when the land becomes just another commodity—and when ghosts themselves must adapt to new ways and ring up the living on telephones. *The Weir* confronts and urges us to question the assumption that culture and understanding arrive only with electricity and tourists and urbanites. It explores and revitalizes the potentials of storytelling and, by directly confronting earlier modes of spiritualism, revitalizes their energies and brings them to bear on contemporary life. It is also about space and about change and about the changes brought to our understandings of interior and exterior spaces when they are invaded by new forces that may not initially seem to belong.

Whether any of these characters believes the tales of spirit rapping, in a literal sense, matters less than the fact they have a space (partly found and partly created) in which they belong and may share not just stories about the surrounding area but also the pain and confusion and unpredictable agonies of their lives. Language is no longer so specifically regional; the only nurturing family is the manufactured one created by patrons of the bar; the child is dead. The space for communion may be small and the communion itself temporary. But there is a space and there is communion.

CHAPTER 3

Travelling in Place

Marina Carr's *By the Bog of Cats* . . . (1998)

> Representation becomes the auratic process by which a place that had been misrepresented or not represented at all finally achieves presence.
> —Seamus Deane, "The Production of Cultural Space in Irish Writing"

At the heart of Marina Carr's play *By the Bog of Cats* . . . (1998) lies an irony: Hester Swane, a member of the Travelling community, has lifelong roots and a deeper, more mystical tie to place than is evident in any member of the "settled" community with which she is frequently in conflict. Carr's handling of geographic space is not the simple reversal that such an irony might suggest, however. Rather, it is complex, shifting, ambiguous. The Midlands bog of the title, a quintessentially Irish place, becomes a space for exploration and assessment of Irish cultural anxieties and conflicts about family, gender, ethnicity, class, and relationship to the land. Hester is simultaneously Irish and other, at home in the bog yet alienated from most of the local residents. Carr's minimal staging is painterly and mystical, allowing audiences to enter a magical space where the dichotomy of Hester's belonging (and not belonging) works itself out. To use Henri Lefebvre's terms, space in this play is not "the passive locus of social relations" but an "active" space, underlying and supporting "hegemonies" of power.[1]

By the Bog of Cats . . . opens on the bog of the title, and many (perhaps most) productions have followed the text's implication that the opening scene should be staged impressionistically:[2] "Dawn . . . A bleak white landscape of ice and snow. Music, a lone violin. Hester Swane trails the corpse of a black swan after her, leaving a trail of blood in the snow."[3] The audience's first glimpse of Hester comes in a minimally representative landscape, at a moment that could be dawn or dusk. Like Maureen O'Hara emerging from the misty landscape in John Ford's iconic film *The Quiet Man* (1952), Hester is a woman immediately associated visually with the natural world in which she is so comfortable. Carr specifies that Hester's entrance is accompanied by violin music, a sound that Western culture has trained us to associate with pleasant romanticism. The presence of the dead swan, though, is the first of many indications that while Hester is tied to the landscape she is not the sweet Irish colleen of myth and legend, and this will not be a romantic evocation of a rural Irish homeland.

The use of color here is startling and powerful. Black and a trail of red stand out against the starkly white background. The opening also suggests a particular way in which audiences must engage with the bog. Inevitably, of course, the stage will be a sort of liminal space, a representation of the "real" bog, but not the bog itself. That would be the case even if the text suggested a more naturalistic evocation, complete with representational topography and vegetation. In other plays—*The Mai* (1994), *On Raftery's Hill* (2000), and *Ariel* (2002), for example—Carr has used much more naturalistic sets. *By the Bog of Cats* . . . , though, is as minimalist and as painterly as the opening of *Waiting for Godot*, or as the opening of Act Two in Carr's *Portia Coughlin* (1996), when the drowned Portia (who also has Traveller roots) is raised out of the river and "suspended there, dripping water, river algae, frogspawn, waterlilies" while the ghost of Gabriel stands "aloof" and sings.[4] The opening of *By the Bog of Cats* . . . is a lush conjuration not of naturalistic details but of the emotional feel of the bog. The *Macbeth*-like opening of Act Two, in which the bloodied ghost of Joseph Swane appears next to the long white tablecloth of the wedding feast, repeats the palette and the use of musical background that is so dominant at the start of Act One. Those magical, vague sets are linked to the emotional reality of the bog and to the emotional reality of those who live by or on it—those who belong to this natural space and those who would change it.

Like many Irish plays, *By the Bog of Cats* . . . has traveled well. Different audiences invariably understand it differently, but Carr's opening conjures an image in sharp contrast to the image likely to be in the minds of audience members familiar with the vast level mud plains of Irish bogs denuded by mechanical harvesting of turf and characterized by perilous muddy trenches. Those far less appealing bog images are foregrounded in films like *Eat the Peach* (1986) and *I Went Down* (1997, with a screenplay by Conor McPherson), both of which were filmed in the Midlands Bog of Allen. Carr's bog has apparently not been stripped commercially, and audiences are plunged into a necessarily imaginative understanding of it, underscored by the immediate revelation that only a native like Hester can easily distinguish dawn from dusk in this world that is "always shiftin' and changin' and coddin' the eye" (267). The impressionistic option is theatrically practical, since staging becomes primarily a matter of lighting. It is also dramatically effective, using music to underscore the mood and capturing attention quickly without requiring the audience to note details of a representational set. In Eli Rozik's terms, this is an "imagistic" stage convention that both minimizes and distorts elements of the literal setting. That convention "compensates" for the impossibility that the stage could fully describe the bog and makes major "contributions . . . to the description of a fictional world."[5] As director Garry Hynes has put it, Carr is "not bound by naturalism, [but] has a poetic world of her own."[6] The set of *By the Bog of Cats* . . . indeed functions poetically, adding crucial nonverbal, nonlinear information to audience perceptions of the play's world.

This opening suggests the extent to which most audience members, like most characters in the play, are outsiders in this world. The bog is as out of range for other characters and for most audiences as a house (even her own house, where she has "never felt at home") is for Hester. Imagining how this narrative would change if set in any of the urban areas where Travellers and settled people rub, often abrasively, against each other emphasizes the importance of Carr's bog setting. Like the 1992 Irish film *Into the West* (not to be confused with the U.S. television series of the same name), *By the Bog of Cats* . . . is able to present rural Traveller culture with a veneer of romanticism precisely because it is so distant from the urban realities of most audience members.

The play particularizes the general locale Carr has chosen for many of her plays, exploring her native Irish Midlands, geography largely unmapped and unvisited in Irish drama. If on one level Carr is presenting an actual landscape, on another perhaps more significant level she is creating, with the audience's help, a landscape that demands to be entered imaginatively, not "realistically." She has repeatedly described the Midlands as a "crossroads" and landscape as "another character in the work."[7] Situated between the gritty Dublin urbanscape and the green West of peasant Ireland, the Midlands are an ambiguous interior landscape, which could be interpreted as feminized and where inhabitants speak with their own challenging accent. Carr describes this accent as "a lot flatter and rougher and more guttural than the written word allows" (261), and it is a key factor in establishing the play's locale, planting events firmly in the Midlands and triggering from the outset an understanding that this world is neither Dublin nor the Aran Isles. Played off against the standard Hiberno-English dialect that has a powerful hold on aural memory and constitutes a far milder variation of "standard" English, the Midlands dialect acknowledges the worth of the regional and implies skepticism about authority in both language and culture. Carr has described it as "more rebellious than the written word permits."[8]

Carr's play establishes the central importance not only of the Midlands but also of the bog, one of those swampy areas famous for preserving odd fragments of the Irish past and posing real dangers in both past and present, particularly for outsiders. Bogs are not unique to Ireland, but they are bound up with the island's economics, environmental concerns, and sociohistory. The play balances this Midlands bog against the equally ambiguous Cassidy farmhouse, which is neither an Ascendency big house nor the familiar Abbey Theatre peasant cottage. A central question facing Irish handling of bogs—what is to be developed and what is to be preserved?—parallels central questions facing these characters and Irish culture. Who belongs and who does not? What things and people should be acknowledged or welcomed as essentially Irish?

Though Hester's community is now commonly termed the "Travelling" community, other characters invariably refer to her as a "tinker," a term that is generally regarded (and that these characters clearly regard) as pejorative and largely dismissive of the value of Traveller culture. The question whether Travellers constitute an ethnic minority, a culture, a lifestyle choice, or a temporary response to poverty is complex, and conclusions about the most appropriate way to describe Travellers (or even whether the term should be capitalized) lie beyond the scope of this consideration.[9] Carr's Midlands community, however, clearly regards Travellers as a distinct and identifiable group—and as a group whose way of life must be (as Hester puts it) "eradicated" as part of Ireland's reformulation of cultural identity. Carr notes that she made Hester a Traveller "because travellers are our national outsiders aren't they?"[10] The name "Traveller" itself is a reminder that one thing separating Travellers from the settled community is their relationship to space. Hester, a Traveller who does not travel, is thus separate from both Traveller and settled communities; she emerges as an outsider with an instinctive and unselfconscious attachment to the bog, rooted in her own biography. For audiences, the appeal of Hester and her bog is likely to involve the fact that the bog is a site where Hester can resist dominant contemporary Irish mores.

Clichéd realities of Traveller experience pepper the dialogue. Hester prefers life in a caravan to life in a house. Xavier, a settled farmer, threatens to run her off, as he claims to have run her mother off before her. When Hester burns the house, Monica observes in horror, "That's what the tinkers do, isn't it, burn everythin' after them?" (322)—a reference to the Traveller tradition of disposing (preferably by burning) of the possessions of those who have died. Or, consider the implications buried in the following exchange:

> Mrs. Kilbride: A waste of time givin' chances to a tinker. All tinkers understands is the open road and where the next bottle of whiskey is comin' from.
> Monica: Well, you should know and your own grandfather wan!
> Mrs. Kilbride: My grandfather was a wanderin' tinsmith—
> Monica: And what's that but a tinker with notions! (314–15)

Mrs. Kilbride, who refers to her grandfather as "wandering" rather than "travelling," believes tinkers lack ambition and possess a fondness for whiskey. Her distinction between tinkers and tinsmiths raises the much-debated issue of whether tinkers became a separate culture primarily because earning their living by mending tin goods required that they wander. Most interestingly, she reveals discomfort about her own position as a product of assimilation, which was Irish government policy toward Travellers for several decades in the late twentieth century. Mrs. Kilbride's insistence that her grandfather was not a tinker signals her eagerness to obscure her links to a community she believes is inferior. Her insistence (despite evidence afforded by her grandfather's experience) that it is a waste of time to give tinkers a chance (a "tinker's chance"?) suggests that she too has come to regard them as an ethnic group. If being a tinker is a lifestyle choice (either voluntary or induced by poverty), then possibilities for change might be more likely than if tinkers are an ethnic group.[11]

Hester may be a tinker, but her association with the Bog of Cats is intimate and lifelong. Although her lover has built her a house beside the bog, she is never seen in the interior of that house, and her relationship to the bog illustrates the ancient Irish tradition of *dinnseanchas*, the lore of places that "knows" them not just by name and location but by history and experience. She simply wishes to live in proximity to the bog and says early on that she would rather die than leave the Bog of Cats. She retains an unfettered independence, living fiercely outside the cultural pale, unknown and exotic, able to see ghosts and connect with wild swans. The bog has created and shaped her. It is the environment that becomes her destiny, since she belongs to it but not to the surrounding community.

Hester Swane is a Traveller and an unwed mother—abandoned by her mother, by her father, and by the father of her child. In a world increasingly prone to weigh individual and cultural worth on a commercial scale, her zero bank balance is regularly contrasted with the assets of others. In a world concerned with family bonds, Hester's missing parents are balanced by the overly present parents of Carthage and Caroline. In the end, having murdered her beloved child, Hester is herself dead by the Bog of Cats. But it is Hester—and perhaps only Hester—who has truly lived in this drama, and she is by no means simply a victim. Her vital, passionate presence is so vivid that productions must be careful lest other characters fade into the background.

Spectators who in real life might try to remove her daughter from Hester's charge are likely to find themselves siding with her in the parental dispute about custody. Here, as elsewhere in both history and literature, a child is the locus of struggle between cultures. The child's father and grandmother both cite "saving" her as a justification for destroying her mother. One of the compelling ironies in the play, then, is that audiences are likely to side with Hester, in opposition to the settled middle-class norm to which most of them undoubtedly belong and that has typically sought to "rescue" the children of cultural groups deemed inferior by assimilating those children into the dominant group.[12] A similar irony occurs in Frank McGuinness's *Gates of Gold*, when members of a theater audience likely to be middle class and at least nominally straight are engaged sympathetically with gay characters. In both plays, mainstream audiences who "belong" are encouraged to depart from their own norms to engage with those who might be termed native outsiders.

Both plays exemplify what Eli Rozik has described as the ability of a performance text to become a mechanism that "manipulates the audience into a preconceived perspective on a fictional world . . . subvert[ing] established values and beliefs."[13] The conflagration, murder, and suicide at the end of the play could be seen as confirmations of value systems that ostracize and destroy nonconformists, but that is not the major impact. The order restored does not seem desirable, and the results fail to satisfy the (non-mainstream) values Carr has led the audience to embrace. Hester's survival skills are not up to the task of defying the community, and she pays a large price for her nonconformity. At least momentarily, though, it might seem better not to belong to the society that has rejected her.

Hester's Traveller status is not the only quality that creates a gulf between her and the settled community. Her ease with ghosts and ghost fanciers—ephemera invisible to other characters—reveals contrasting notions of "realistic" and "magic" understandings. In words reminiscent of the mad Ophelia, Hester notes that she knows "where the best bog rosemary grows and the sweetest wild bog rue" (314). Her love of the bog across which she wanders at night and from which she cannot imagine being separated indicates a notion of the relationship between humans and nature that is very different than the notion held by farmers who labor during daylight hours to control, shape, and make "productive" the land they believe they own. The competing identities of characters are expressed in their alternate relationships to space.

Above all, it is Hester's sexuality that disturbs the surrounding community. She is not promiscuous, as Traveller stereotype suggests she will be, but she is certainly enthusiastically and openly sexual,[14] and (like women in many minority groups) she has been exoticized, so that other characters find her simultaneously seductive and threatening. Her lustiness is revealed not only by her unwed motherhood but also by the openness with which she discusses sex, bragging about what she has taught Carthage and about their mutual sexual pleasure. Dialogue regularly emphasizes Hester's warmth and "toughness" in contrast to the coldness and softness of Caroline, her ultimately successful rival for Carthage. Caroline's father uses a stereotypically emblematic gun not only to insist on his power to control land and family but also to threaten Hester's life (holding the gun to her throat) and to threaten her sexually (using it to look down her dress). He would not behave this way with a woman in his own community—not only because none of them would defy him, but also because he would regard such behavior as unacceptable in the settled community and because he finds the women in his world less sexually exciting.

Bogs are powerful territories in contemporary Ireland as well as Irish history. Contemporary drainage of the bogs and the mechanized commercial harvesting of their peat to provide fuel for both private homes and electricity generation are endangering their very existence. John Wilson Foster has noted their importance as emblems of the steady retreat of wild nature in the face of cultivation. Foster also reminds us that in the seventeenth century the bogs were associated with wild, resistant Irish who defied the English. The "unregenerate" bogs were sanctuaries for the "unregenerate" Irish who retreated there to avoid the invading English.[15] "Bog Irish," then, may be either a compliment or a critique, depending on the accent with which it is uttered. Seamus Heaney's well-known concentration on Irish bogs presents them as preservers of Irish history, myth, artifacts, and often human bodies.[16] The Bog of Cats around which Hester Swane's life revolves is a site that illustrates Wordsworth's recognition in "Lines: Composed a Few Miles above Tintern Abbey" that we both perceive and "half create" the world. The bog is a common resource, but characters in this play—like characters in real life—disagree about how it should be used. Like Hester, it is simultaneously beautiful, unknown, unpredictable, mysterious, compelling, dangerous. Like the Travelling community to which Hester belongs, the bog's very existence threatens and is threatened by forces of contemporary life. It is a place where contending values and approaches to life play out their differences. It is also a site from which Hester can mount a rebellion against cultural standardization that is as clear and as doomed to defeat as the rebellion against standardization in Brian Friel's *Translations*.

Dialogue and stage directions indicate that Hester's caravan at the edge of the bog is visible, and stage directions specify that she should sit on the caravan steps and go inside for a bottle of wine. How much, if any, of the caravan should be visible to the audience is an important question. If it is visible, what does it look like? Is it the more visually romantic horse-drawn caravan of the early twentieth century,[17] or the less visually appealing modern replacement, a camper or trailer? If the audience can see the caravan, then it—like the exterior of Hester's house and the interior of the Cassidy house, which are central to later scenes—is a somewhat more familiar space for most audience members. If it is not visible (as it was not in the premiere) then the vagueness of the setting facilitates the audience's entry into the play's ghost world and the overwhelming mystery of the opening is heightened. In either case, mystery sets a context for everything that follows. The mystery is not limited to the way the bog is represented on stage, but the play's handling of space suggests relationships of crucial importance to both characters and events.

The light of flames from the burning house in Act Three is as visually powerful as the opening of Act One. Carr might have balanced the minimalist set with verbal evocations of the bog, allowing her characters to parallel those of Friel and McPherson in describing things audiences cannot see. For the most part she has not opted to do so. "The Black Swan" song ("to be recorded and used during the play") describes the swan sleeping

> On the bank of grey water,
> Hidden in a nest of leaves
> So none can disturb her. (263)

And Hester's closing words to Carthage, which feel a bit like Christy's wooing of Pegeen in Synge's *The Playboy of the Western World*, give an additional verbal image of the bog: "When all of this is over or half remembered and you think you've almost forgotten me again, take a walk along the Bog of Cats and wait for a purlin' wind through your hair or a soft breath be your ear or a rustle behind ya. That'll be me and Josie ghostin' ya" (340). In general, though, the absence of naturalistic detail on the set is accompanied by an absence of verbal descriptions.

Other recent Irish plays that use both interior and exterior space employ techniques that illuminate by contrast what Carr does here. Brian Friel's *Dancing at Lughnasa* (1990) and Frank McGuinness's *Dolly West's Kitchen* (1999), for example, use single sets that include both interiors and exteriors. The interiors are somewhat more realistic than the exteriors, and characters cross the boundaries between spaces. In McGuinness's *The Bird Sanctuary* (1994), the Bootersdown Marsh represents an in-between area, a boundary between human and nonhuman, between shore and land, that is as sacred to some characters as the bog is to Hester. *The Bird*

Sanctuary, though, is set in an interior, restricted world, and neither audience nor protagonist visits the marsh. The reach of the space is extended beyond the set because flowers and weeds from the marsh are brought inside, because the colors of the interior (including the paint splotches on clothes) are the same as those of the marsh, and because the set is dominated by a large painting of the marsh. Stage directions call for the set's rear wall to dissolve at the end of *The Bird Sanctuary*, "magically" revealing the marsh.[18] The set of *By the Bog of Cats* . . . functions very differently, despite its comparable middle territory. Interior and exterior spaces are not seen simultaneously, and there is no ultimate linking of these disparate places. Just as the maps in *Translations* and the photographs in *The Weir* do not reproduce the "real world," but instead establish a shaped perspective on that world, the set of *By the Bog of Cats* . . . is a manipulation of space aimed at setting a context within which the play's action must be viewed.

Carr's renegotiation of stereotypes of space and gender is illuminated by comparing this play with Euripides's *Medea* and with Nathaniel Hawthorne's *The Scarlet Letter*, both of which influenced *By the Bog of Cats*. . . . The fifth-century (BC) play and the nineteenth-century American novel present women in conflict with their cultures, and with their lovers—the same conflicts that animate Carr's play. The parallels add a non-twentieth-century, non-Irish shadow to a very Irish play, and Carr's renegotiation of relationships between various times and texts illuminates her use of space.

Carr has repeatedly noted that her play is based on *Medea*, and *By the Bog of Cats* . . . is one of a number of contemporary Irish plays (by, among others, Seamus Heaney, Brendan Kennelly, and Tom Paulin) that recast Greek drama in the Irish idiom, frequently with the intent of throwing a revealing light on Irish history and politics.[19] Carr's use of Greek drama is not confined to a narrow understanding of politics as sectarian violence and colonial or postcolonial relationships. It focuses on the more personal politics of gender and ethnic issues, but it shares what J. Michael Walton has identified as a central aspect of Medea, who becomes "the supreme metaphor for oppression, because it is the supreme taboo [the killing of her children] that she violates."[20] Carr's Hester exemplifies the rage not of a nation oppressed by another nation, but of a woman and a Traveller oppressed in her homeland, a metaphoric outcast in the very space where she feels she most belongs.

M. K. Martinovich, describing the production of *By the Bog of Cats* . . . that she directed for Irish Repertory of Chicago in 2001, suggests that Carr's use of interior and exterior spaces resembles the standard Greek use of inside and outside. Both Hester and Medea, she concludes, "are in a sense ultimately destroyed by their need to belong to . . . outer realms" instead of remaining content in interior, feminine space.[21] Enrica Cerquoni notes similar connections with the spaces inhabited by the Noras of Synge and Ibsen—females seeking to "release themselves" from "claustrophobic interior space."[22] Hanna Scolnicov examines women and interior space throughout theatrical history, and she too often likens the association to house arrest or prison.[23] If interior space is feminine space, however, it is only because men (like the collection of male playwrights whom these analysts consider) have so designated it.

The case for exterior space as masculine space is far stronger when the exterior space is urban than when it is not. The modern city generally restricts women's activities to daylight hours in "safe" places in the company of men; city streets are male territory, which is why literature may feature a *flâneur* but not a *flâneuse*.[24] The "social maps" for men and women are different, especially in urban areas.[25] When exterior space is the natural world, though, a different pattern predominates: "Woven everywhere into the tapestry of European art and literature and seemingly an inseparable part of most philosophical and scientific texts . . . is the assumption that women are closer to nature than men are. The notion is not intended as a compliment . . . The idea that women are close to nature is an argument for the dominion of men."[26] Hester Swane's bog—like Hester Prynne's New England wilderness—is space that resists male dominance and control, allowing for greater physical and intellectual freedom.

Annette Kolodny and Gillian Rose have persuasively considered attitudes toward the land as examples of gender differences. The masculine gaze of explorers and settlers is analogous to "rape" of the land, and males fear that the "terrifying" feminized landscapes will unman them.[27] Hester's connection to swan and bog are repeatedly emphasized, and the association of women with nature is incorporated in language that supports this view of women and landscape. Caroline insists that Carthage has "built [Hester] up from the ground" when he seeks to integrate her into his community (283). Carthage threatens to "mow" down Hester (290). Xavier suggests he will "plough" through her, and he connects Carthage's inability to "control a mere woman" to an inability to control the farm (332). Any easy division of interior and exterior space into feminine and masculine space is further complicated by the fact that the bog, shrouded by falling snow in the opening scene, for example, can seem as constricted as interior space. Despite the fact that the bog is Hester's territory (and also comfortable terrain for Catwoman and Monica Murray), exterior space is not exclusively feminine space in this play, and the gender stereotypes of space are complicated rather than reversed.

The fondness of Irish playwrights for interior space has often gone hand-in-hand with Irish political, sexual, and social subordination of women, who were confined to interior spaces by both church and state, as exemplified by the 1937 Irish constitution.[28] Hester, however, is not seeking to escape interior space. She has simply refused to inhabit it, despite her yearning to make a conventional life with Carthage. She has never lived in the home he built for her, and she often abandons even her caravan for the bog. The extent to which the exterior space of Motherland may be seen as women's natural space—a reality that may frighten men—emerges in parallels between Carr's play and Hawthorne's novel. Like Hawthorne's Hester Prynne, Hester Swane lives on the outskirts of the civilization whose rules she has flaunted, and civilization associates her with the natural area where she roams—her personal wildness thrives in uncultivated geographic areas; her sexuality is as untamed and uncontrolled as the bog she makes her home.[29] Hawthorne's Hester has been cast out by a patriarchal society horrified at her lack of chastity and convinced that her unruliness has been sanctioned and encouraged by the unruly wilderness surrounding their Puritan society. Carr's Hester has lived by the uncultivated space of the bog since birth, but both she and her daughter are also products of what her patriarchal society sees as sexual transgression. One result is her increased isolation, particularly given the fact that her mother—like so many dramatic Irish mothers—has failed her.

Carr and Hawthorne use similar color palettes, patterning black and white with accents of red.[30] The Hesters are at the bottoms of their communities' power scales. And Catwoman's prediction that Carthage and Caroline will have "separate tombstones" brings to mind the fate of Hawthorne's Hester and Dimmesdale who, unable to share a life, are granted a single tombstone. The gender patterning of Carr's play varies from that of Hawthorne's novel. In *The Scarlet Letter*, a woman is caught between a passionate man not her husband and the dull pedant who is. In Carr's play a man chooses to abandon his passionate lover in favor of the dull conformist who becomes his wife. Arguably, Dimmesdale's choice of conventional religious values over his passion for Hester is as clear an indication of conformity as is Carthage's choice, but to this reader it seems more complex. Carr's use of Hawthorne's novel has no other precedent in Irish drama that I know of and adds additional layers to a remapping of literature that is as intriguing as her remapping of Irish geography and stage space. The patterning of black and white in the opening scene might also be read as a kind of writing, a visual reference to Carr's "rewriting" of earlier texts from very different territories.[31]

The first and third acts of *By the Bog of Cats . . .* are set outside, by the bog. Sandwiched between them in the second act is the interior of the Cassidy farmhouse, which could be anywhere. Delineated thus briefly the settings may seem starkly contrasted—and may seem a disruption of the common stereotypes that identify contained space as space where women belong and extended space as space where they do not. It is Hester, after all, who is inextricably linked to the extended space of the bog and who seems and feels "out of place" when she is inside.

Hester dreams her missing mother will return to the bog to "see me life was complete, that I had Carthage and Josie and me own house" (336). The life Hester dreams of building approximates the more conventional life represented by the farmhouse. Seeking to belong, she at least partially gives in to her culture's pressure to define herself as others would have her defined, attempting to replicate conventional cultural notions of home, woman, and family. Hester's murder of her brother has left her and Carthage with enough money to buy land and build a house where she may act out social norms. Land and house move them ever closer to the lifestyle of the Cassidys, despite Hester's dismissal of the Cassidy life as "a few lumpy auld acres and notions of respectability" (289). It is respectability that Hester will never be able to attain. As Carthage informs her, "It's not in your power—Look, I'm up to me neck in another life that can't include ya any more" (289). Nevertheless, the forces of domesticity associated with interior space are invading the bog, and it is only after the wedding, when Hester is forced to give up on her dream of a life with Carthage, that she burns down the house, maintaining "it should never have been built in the first place. Let the bog have it back. Never liked that house anyway" (322). Houses are not always homes, and houses can burn. The bog endures, and in the end, Hester, like the stereotypical tinker itinerant, remains beyond the capitalist nexus of the Cassidys.

The permeability of the border between confined space and extended space allows traffic in both directions, providing a visual reinforcement of the plot's demonstration that boundaries are artificial and difficult to preserve. The farmhouse is Caroline Cassidy's territory and thus might seem typical woman's space, particularly because ever since the late seventeenth century, domestic space has been regarded as "non-productive,"[32] a term the Cassidys would undoubtedly also apply to the bog. Like the surrounding farmland, the house has been molded by patriarchal imperatives. Interior, domesticated space remains "safer" (all the murders and violent deaths—Hester's brother, Xavier's son, Josie, Hester—take place outside), but it is susceptible to penetration by the errant forces of the bog. Caroline (a weak, asexual creature likely to please the arbiters of both religious and political "norms" for women[33]) expects to celebrate her marriage within the safe haven provided by the farmhouse. Throughout the wedding reception, however, those connected to the bog invade this sanctuary, dragging the values, history, sights, and smells of the bog inside—just as the house Carthage built for Hester sought to drag settled values into the space of the bog.

The farmhouse wedding reception is invaded by Catwoman, who deliberately flaunts conventional customs and manners, and by the ghost of Joseph Swane, an ethereal presence who bears witness to Hester's and Carthage's violent past and whose bloodied figure echoes both that of the swan in the opening scene and the ghost of Banquo in *Macbeth*. The link between the ghost and the Ghost Fancier suggests that spirits can transgress the boundaries of "interior" and "exterior" space, diminishing the meaning of such terms.

Carthage's name brings another connection into the play and emphasizes the postcolonial elements evident if we read backward through the house and the bog to a tale of English domination of

Ireland. Carthage's name is a glancing reference to the metaphor of Ireland as Carthage, dominated and destroyed first by Rome and then by the Arabs.[34] As Frank McGuinness (whose own play *Carthaginians* also uses the reference) put it in the program note for the opening production of Carr's play: "Carthage must be destroyed, but what happens to the destroyers?"[35] Dido, legendary founder of Carthage, threw herself on a burning pyre in agony at Aeneas's forced departure. Hester's actions and fate are reminiscent of Medea's and Dido's. The city of Carthage is destroyed by fire, just as Hester destroys by fire the house Carthage built for her but now attempts to claim for himself. The fate of feminine Ireland, in the hands of a masculine colonizer whose power is a result of violence driven by greed and envy, casts a suggestive illumination on the issues of sexual and cultural domination that are Carr's main focus. The masculine force in *Bog* is native, not colonial, but it is linked to the aspirational acquisitiveness of Celtic Tiger Ireland, whose capitalist orientation seemed to many to have swept in from elsewhere. Hester's function, then, is linked to the one Mary Burke associates with the "Revival fashion for depicting tinkers as the antithesis of the expanding Irish bourgeoisie and the speakers of truth to the powers of land ownership, religiosity, and conservatism."[36]

Monica Frawley's set design for the Abbey Theatre's premiere production emphasized the fluidity of space in the world of the play. Opting not to fully represent the interior space of Act Two, Frawley situated the wedding table on one edge of the bog. The caravan was not visible on stage. Olwen Fouéré, who created the role of Hester for that production, has explained that she felt she was inhabiting stage space divided between "Hester's more personal territory" and "her larger landscape." Since the larger landscape was stage left, "where an audience looks first . . . you could theorize that, at the beginning of the play, the audience and the people from the town share the same world . . . and Hester is the intruder . . . But Hester's territory moves . . . , drawing the audience with her, so towards the end of the play Hester shares her world with the audience." Since eventually "the world of the town came in on her, driving her out,"[37] we could also theorize that the audience's awareness of Hester's outsider status was heightened, because by this time the production located the audience in the same space as Hester.

This conception of the play's fluid, minimalist space as divided into distinct but overlapping areas is a more sophisticated example of the divided space used in Carr's early play *Low in the Dark* (1989), in which "The men's space" is balanced by a "Bizarre bathroom" that is clearly women's space.[38] In both plays, the apparently divided space is used to challenge assumptions that the world is as neatly ordered as the division implies, and characters penetrate the worlds of the other. The bog's "meaning" is inextricable from the perceptions of people who experience it, in reality or in its stage representation. For Fouéré, thinking back on the requirements of playing Hester, "The interior landscape of the bog, the colours of rage and passionate love. This place is dark, deep, and conversant with the world at its most reduced and primal, a place of great anguish and great exultation."[39]

The most dramatic visual in Act Two involves a patterning as powerful as that which opened the play. Inside the Cassidy house, a long table covered with a white cloth is ready for the wedding feast. Caroline is there in her white bridal gown. Josie wears her white communion dress, because her mother has not bought her a dress for the wedding. The appropriately named Mrs. Kilbride is inappropriately dressed in what looks like a wedding gown, because "How was I supposed to know the bride'd be wearin' white as well" (309). These white dresses foreshadow Hester's dramatic appearance, wearing the white gown Carthage had brought her nine years earlier when he hoped to marry her, and declaring that her place as rightful bride has been usurped. Patrick Lonergan finds a link between Hester's "ruined wedding dress" and Miss Havisham in Dickens's *Great Expectations*,[40] but the text does not specify that Hester's dress is ruined, and it is the overall visual image of this farmhouse that matters most. Four white dresses and a white tablecloth gleam on stage, absorbing the available light and spilling it back against the darkness of the surrounding characters and backdrop. The inevitable effect of these whites was heightened in the opening production because the other wedding guests were generally dressed in dark colors. This compelling pattern of white against darkness suggests the existence of commonalities among the women wearing white and contributes to the scene's development of other important themes. Mrs. Kilbride has already noted that this is a "glorious white winter's day" (304). First Mrs. Kilbride and then Josie pose with Carthage, in postures that provide each of them with a bridelike role given here to neither Caroline, who takes the photos, nor Hester. Those images reinforce the dialogue's frequent suggestion of inappropriate sexual relationships between a variety of parents and children. In a line reminiscent of Carr's early use of absurdist comic devices, Hester remarks that Mrs. Kilbride's criticism of Hester's white dress is "The kettle callin' the pot white" (312). The role of photography here, and when Mrs. Kilbride photographs her shoes, invites comparison with the role of photographs in *The Weir*. These momentarily frozen moments function much like tableaux. They are attempts to capture a permanent image of "truth," providing another visual, nonlinear image focused on issues not addressed in the dialogue.

The white dresses signal not only commonalities but also a destabilized world order. Roland Barthes has analyzed at length the extent to which "Fashion behaves like language itself," projecting the self-definitions of the bodies wearing the clothing.[41] The three women in white in this scene have chosen their attire, much as they choose the words they speak. The visually powerful presence of the white-clad "brides" shatters any conviction that the meaning of white is clear or definite. Who belongs in white and is the "real" bride? What is the relationship between the communion dress worn by so many Irish girls like Josie and the wedding dress that so many Irish women hope to wear?[42] In Carr's *On Raftery's Hill* (2000), Shalome's entrance wearing the wedding dress intended for her granddaughter provides a similar visual communication of themes (in that case, themes that swirl quite openly around incest). Carr's mastery of theater's spatial and visual possibilities is illustrated by the translation of complex themes into unforgettable visual images. The whites in this scene are as powerful as the opening representation of the bog and are equally effective as nonverbal methods of denaturalizing our expectations.

Carr provides minimal specifics about sets and clothing, but those she does provide suggest a monochromatic palette of black, white, and gray—broken startlingly by streaks of red. In the opening scene Hester drags black wing (the dead swan) behind her through a snow storm, leaving a trail of blood. Joseph's blood-covered ghost in Act Two and the bloody knife with which Hester kills first Josie and then herself in Act Three provide for those acts' comparable accents of red. The sunrise and sunset time frames offer opportunities for the intrusion of red light, as does the fire Hester sets. (In the Chicago Irish Repertory production, red was added to Josie's costume to symbolize her as "sacrificial lamb."[43])

Hester Swane's transgressive appearance in a wedding dress within the celebratory domestic space of this play (where she does not belong) demands that the characters and the audience compare her to Caroline, and the spaces they inhabit are also juxtaposed. Carthage may have chosen Caroline over Hester, but he hardly respects his bride, and no passion for her is evident in his words or behavior. Even Caroline's father, who refers to her as a "whiny little rip" (331), neither respects nor likes her, and Caroline herself accepts Hester's assertion that Caroline has been "broken" (337) by her father. Hester seems equally correct in asserting that Caroline will never stand up for anyone or anything against the men in her life. To the men, though, Caroline seems preferable to Hester because she is less of a threat—more conventional, more contemporary, more socially acceptable, more willing to be confined, less mysteriously in touch with her natural environment, less defiant, less sexual. The confrontation with Hester, in which Xavier's gun becomes both sexual threat and life threat, is an instance of male resistance and fear when confronted with female sexuality and independence. It is the same resistance and fear that drive Carthage from Hester to Caroline. In the end, Carthage's fear of being unmanned by Hester's terrifying sexuality (inseparable from the generous landscape she refuses to leave) sends him rushing from wild bog to cultivated farm, from the uncontrollable woman who loves him with abandon and refuses to be confined by convention, to a young bride already as domesticated as her father's acres. Hester might be seen as an individual incarnation of Matthew Arnold's notion that the Irish are feminine, "romantic and attractive . . . [but] undisciplinable, anarchical and turbulent."[44] A more pertinent connection is probably with the mythic figures of Maeve and Grania, violent and vibrant women who were rejected by Revivalists seeking to reassert Irish masculinity (which they felt had been diminished by British colonial attitudes) in part by specifying a subordinate role for women.[45] Carr embraces Hester's vibrancy and reveals the weakness in the nationalist notion of gender roles—but she does not minimize the cost to Hester and her daughter of defying patriarchal norms.

Contrasted settings are key elements in the play's exploration of issues of life and power, and characters are in large part defined by the extent to which they belong in the play's contrasted spaces. How these settings will be represented on stage is a key production decision. Both are sites of sexual and cultural conflict. From the opening moments, when Hester drags the bleeding corpse of a black swan over a white landscape, the bog's space is quite literally marked by blood and death but also by mythical allusion. The bog is a magical space, as exotic as Hester herself, where ghosts and lovers seek recognition and vengeance, and where hastily buried passions are unearthed and ignited. The scale of the characters' feelings, mirrored in the diesel-fueled conflagration Hester starts, suggests that realistic set pieces are not required and are probably not desirable. The play opens at dawn and closes at dusk, both times that mark the threshold between day and night. By extension, the bog—already an in-between landscape that is neither wet lake nor dry farmland—which is bathed in the particular light of early morning and early evening, perches precariously on the border between rationality and mystery, order and chaos, life and death. Like Beckett's use of deliberately nonspecific space,[46] Carr's mystical bog is generalized on stage. Unlike his space, hers is simultaneously and specifically Irish. An open stage seems particularly well suited to giving these ideas visual expression, and production decisions to use fog, smoke, and glow from the fire to further emphasize the bog's mystery (and to heighten its contrast with the house) make sense.

Other than those gleaming white accents, Carr provides few clues about the look and the feel of the interior setting. A comparison with her earlier play, *The Mai*, which contains more specific descriptions of the domestic space and its relationship to the natural world outside, shows that this underwriting is not simply a matter of established authorial style. By leaving the farmhouse ambiguous, Carr allows particular productions to conjure it as a site of significant transition in the lives of all the characters. The one described set piece is a banquet table, covered in a lace cloth and adorned with heirloom silver. Weddings are performances linked to cultural identities as rooted in the past as the heirloom silver. In Western drama, wedding celebrations are standard fare, generally signaling closure, reconciliation, and reestablishment of order. But this feast is interrupted and the bride's role is distorted and inconclusive. Exiles from the other world of the bog invade the celebration, refusing to be resettled in any ordered place, and their invasion disrupts the community. Like the exterior setting, the interior demands a kind of indeterminacy and archetypal resonance that does not fit easily with a representational set. But because this space reembodies

Caroline instead of Hester, it is contained, proper, and ultimately less seductive than the bog.

Henri Lefebvre's consideration of the production of space as both social and class-based[47] suggests an important consideration for staging of the wedding banquet. At the start of Act Two, when the table is being set, Catwoman sits alone at center table, where she clearly does not belong. She and Joseph's ghost leave before others arrive, though, and after that Carr provides no details about seating. It seems likely, however, that the bride and groom are seated according to tradition at center table, the place of importance that Catwoman briefly usurped, with the others ranging out from them according to status. When Hester arrives, she never sits down, and it seems unlikely that there is a vacant chair where she could have been seated, since she is not expected. Apparently the waiter is the only other character who does not sit. The banquet scene, then, provides not only a powerful use of white but also a visual representation of the community's social order, of the class of its residents, and of who belongs where.

Hester is an outsider in the farmhouse world of Carr's play partly because of her individual qualities. She is also an outsider and lower class because she is a Traveller, one of Carr's "national outsiders." José Lanters's recent survey of tinkers in Irish literature details the ubiquitous presence of tinkers as "primitive" other (often with tremendous seductive power) in Irish literature. "The notion that beneath the civilized veneer of every modern Irish citizen there lies a 'tinker' core," Lanters reports, "began to emerge in the decades before the creation of the Free State."[49] Travellers, of course, do not respect borders. Their ability to seduce settled people into their way of life means that boundaries are permeable in both directions, and the fluidity of social "place" is reflected in the fluidity of this play's stage space and the difficulty of distinguishing dawn from dusk. Traveller and Settled illuminate each other by contrast in this play, but they also shape shift toward (and away from) each other.

Many of the attitudes and behaviors that put Hester beyond the metaphoric pale are particular problems because she is a woman. Carthage, who is apparently equally lusty and who has fathered Hester's child, is not dismissed (as is Hester) as a "hoor." Nor does the dialogue indicate that Carthage feels any twinges about leaving Hester, displacing her from her home, and moving to take her daughter out of her care, now that he will have a wife to tend the child in a proper domestic space, a home where they belong.

The contrast between Hester and Caroline exists within the framework of a more general stereotypical division of women into categories associated with specific places. It is not so much the virgin-whore division, though there are echoes of that, as the division between dark ladies and light. For many in her community, Hester is simultaneously appealing and repelling—an exotic, mysterious, sultry figure with an ability to tap into the spiritual world of ghosts and witchery and a "savage tinker eye" that frightens people (312). Her sexuality, her association with the wild bog, and her general freedom all tantalize the settled people for whom such freedoms are as unattainable, at least on a permanent basis, as Hester finds the more ordered spaces of their lives. Many of these qualities are associated with Travellers in general, but Hester's gender heightens their impact. As Mary Burke explains it, the Travellers' "alien patina" has often allowed for depiction of "the binary of settled civility/nomadic savagery."[50]

Audience members have the advantage of being more removed from challenging interactions with Travellers than are the characters in this play. For most audiences, Travellers will be far enough away to become exotic and alluring myths. Hester is the most compelling figure in this play, so audiences are led to sympathize with and admire a woman whose sexuality, violence, and mysticism challenge conventions. Ultimately, Hester is not the stereotypical Traveller she has seemed to some commentators.[51] Even her harshest critics, for example, never accuse Hester of littering the landscape or stealing, charges frequently leveled against Travellers.

She is sexual but not promiscuous. Mrs. Kilbride may charge that tinkers understand only the open road, and commentators on the play may refer to Hester as an "itinerant," but in fact the text provides no evidence that Hester has ever been on the road. She spent time at an Industrial School and has otherwise lived where she lives now. Like the majority of real-world Travellers,[52] she is not a literal traveler in the sense of being an itinerant. Rather, she is rooted to the Bog of Cats, a seven-mile-square area from which she cannot imagine being separated. The caravan that she prefers to a house represents the possibility of travel rather than its reality.[53] Hester also lacks the support of the extended family community typical of Traveller life, and so she wanders metaphorically if not literally.[54] Her wandering across the bog indicates her rejection of bourgeois stability rather than either desire for or experience of wider travel.

Hester's very identity is grounded in the space of the bog, not in the space of the house where she has tried to reinvent herself. In the bog she became the woman she is, and there she continues to belong and be most completely herself. The space of the bog has become the place that is the basis of her personal reality and significance. Her link with the land connects her experience with the experience of non-Travellers in this play. "Ah, how can I lave the Bog of Cats," she laments, "everythin' I'm connected to is here. I'd rather die" (273); "I was born on the Bog of Cats and on the Bog of Cats I'll end me days. I've as much right to this place as any of yees, more, for it holds me to it in way it has never held yees" (289). Hester's connection with the swan (Swane/swan), whose life and death shadow and foreshadow her own, is a specific instance of the more general connection between her and the bog.[55] Xavier Cassidy resembles Bull in John B. Keane's *The Field* (1965), both in his scorn for tinkers and in a passion for the land that is as powerful as Hester's love of the bog. Hester may see the bog primarily as "a phenomenon, a space or collection of spaces," but Xavier sees it as the "setting of certain human activities,"[56] and for him those human activities are aimed at financial profit.

Explaining his pleasure that Carthage will marry his daughter, Xavier says, "He loves the land and like me he'd rather die than part with it wance he gets his greedy hands on it" (328). The apparently comparable passions for the land of Hester and Xavier are illuminated by their contrasting contexts. Hester wants only to roam the bog and pick a little bog rue. Certainly she gets plenty of rue, and her mother's song also notes "a heart brimful of rue" (162). As Xavier's reference to "greedy hands" reminds us, he and Carthage are farmers who change and domesticate the land—plowing and planting in expectation of earning a profit. That approach does not eliminate their ability to love the land: as Yi-Fu Tuan points out, "dominance and affection" can coexist in the relationship to place.[57]

Carthage and Xavier rush to save domesticated animals from fire. Hester seems unmoved by the danger to domestic animals. She laments but accepts the death of a wild swan, valuing untamed over domestic animals and accepting the swan's death as part of the natural rhythms of life, which did away with dinosaurs and may destroy them all (267). She does not share the modernizing, utilitarian, "improving" attitude toward nature that marks the settled people. It is a contrast that has played out on a variety of continents, including both North America and Australia, and that has often been used to justify the seizing of territory by western European peoples who would "use" the land as the natives did not and thus "deserve" it more. The contrasts between male farmers and female rue-picker require that we consider what it means to love a piece of land—or perhaps the distinction is between loving land and loving property. Hester may not be a literal itinerant, but the contrast between her attitude toward space and that of others is another sign of the transformed Irish nation from which Carr's plays have emerged. The Travellers' way of life is pitted against and endangered by the more dominant way of life that has surrounded and submerged their subculture—just as Hester's bog is surrounded by an area of increasingly commercialized farms, a world moving into capitalism, emphasizing material possessions, and perfectly willing to make the bogs useful by draining or stripping them. In short, somewhere in the mid-twentieth century, "people's eyes turned away from the country, as a land to be cherished and looked instead to the economy as a source of privilege."[58]

The apparently separate worlds of Travellers and settled people are larded with additional parallel experiences. Monica may associate burning with tinkers, but Mrs. Kilbride threatens to burn Hester out. Perhaps her fondness for burning is a legacy from her grandfather the wandering tinsmith, reflecting the stereotype that a drop of tinker blood makes a tinker? Carthage threatens to take Josie from Hester, but Hester has made the same threat against him. Hester and Caroline are contrasting women, but they are linked by more than their white wedding dresses, since both still yearn for the mothers they lost in their youth,[59] both have dead brothers, and both care for Josie. Tinker violence is matched by non-tinker violence. Hester admits to having killed her brother, but she also suggests that Xavier intentionally killed not only his son's dog but also his son.

By the Bog of Cats . . . is, among other things, a narrative of Midlands resistance to diversity, and Hester recognizes an advantage of her outsider perspective. In recognizing it she invites audiences to share it: "As for me tinker blood, I'm proud of it. It gives me an edge over all of yees around here, allows me see yees for the inbred, underbred, bog-brained shower yees are" (289). Her use of "bog-brained" casts an ironic light on the play's use of the bog's space.

Paula Murphy has pointed out that Carr's culturally specific plays need to be read against the background of the "transformed Irish nation" from which they emerged, for they mirror the "cultural anxiety" evident as Ireland moves into the global community.[60] Contemporary anxieties and displacements have reawakened the long-standing and often unsettling pressure to create a dialogue about what "Irish" means. James Charles Roy, without reference to Carr, has noted an earlier but parallel phenomenon, describing the postindependence "radical breakdown" in Irish affection for and familiarity with the land.[61] Realities of the European Union and the global economy have certainly changed the complexion of the Irish population, directing increased attention toward diversities in Irish life and the resulting, sometimes unpleasant, cultural clashes.[62] The Travelling community to which Hester Swane belongs, however, is a variety of Irishness with an extended history on the island. Long-standing conflicts between the Traveller and settled communities have regularly raised questions of rights and assimilation, of what it means to be "at home" in Ireland. Carr takes a risk in representing a member of this minority community,[63] to which she does not belong. It is the age-old question posed by Frank O'Connor in *The Lonely Voice*: "How if one is not one of the exploited, does one describe them without being one of the exploiters?"[64] Is Carr appropriating the Traveller story? Speaking for people who are increasingly willing and able to speak for themselves? Allowing middle-class theater audiences to indulge in bourgeois voyeurism of both Traveller and Midlands culture? Or, more simply, writing a play (a fiction) that presents dominant and outsider cultures rubbing against each other in the struggle to belong? Regardless of how such questions are answered, remembering the "transformed Irish nation" from which *By the Bog of Cats . . .* emerged allows us to note in the play significant opportunities for dialogue about diversity, about the links between communities, about dominant and repressed values, and about the need to confront any lingering notions of Ireland as a monochromatic, unified homeland.

Many or most of the events in *By the Bog of Cats . . .* could have taken place at any time during the past hundred or hundred and fifty years. The relative absence of specificity contrasts with the more contemporary world of *The Weir*, though both plays state that the time is "the present." Despite mentions of Industrial School, a camera, a bank, and a private hospital, Carr's Midlands are overwhelmingly lacking in references specific to the present.

No one refers to telephones, cars, televisions, or trains; all communication seems face-to-face; all transportation seems to be by foot. A possible reason to avoid visual representation of the caravan is that choosing one sort of caravan (barrel-top wagon or trailer) would suggest a clearer time period. Despite the intrusion of commercialism, this rural Midlands world is so unchanging that the waiter's declared ambition to become an astronaut is a pinprick of surprise—a reminder that this world is both static *and* contemporary. The second edition of the play removed the line in which Caroline noted her early ambition to be "a kindergarten teacher or a air hostess or a beautician."[65] That leaves only becoming an astronaut or death as possible escapes.

Stories take place in both space and time. In obscuring the time of her story and creating a world as unmarked by time as Beckett's vaguely identified settings or Synge's Aran Islands, Carr takes another risk. If Travellers and their settled Midlands neighbors represent a bygone world, then these ghosts have nothing to reveal about our world. The present, though, is inevitably based on the past.[66] Or perhaps the past continues to exist, mingling inextricably with the present. Reading *By the Bog of Cats . . .* against the background of Ireland's current transformations reveals in the play ways of thinking about a variety of Irishness that is long-standing—a traditional diversity. The struggle of these Midlands characters to deal with Hester and her Traveller culture suggests that their own culture is in flux—a world of destabilized values that has much in common with early twenty-first-century Celtic Tiger Ireland and the island's increasingly diverse population. (In the first decade of the twenty-first century, Ireland saw immigration from at least a hundred countries and ethnic groups.[67]) Carr's "unreal" world of ghosts and ghost fanciers thus provides real insights into contemporary realities of culture and identity. The homeland has changed, and those who belong there are an increasingly varied group. Acceptance that Travellers are not outsiders could facilitate understanding that various other others also belong.

For Hester, a fallen woman on the outskirts of conventional space, there is no easy way to resolve the problems of identity and home. Departure does not hold the promise for her that it seemed to offer to characters in earlier plays with similar problems. Ibsen's *A Doll's House*, Synge's *The Playboy of the Western World*, Friel's *Philadelphia, Here I Come!* and *Translations*, McGuinness's *Carthaginians* and *Dolly West's Kitchen* all hold out the possibility that departure from home may be a solution. But Hester is inseparable from the bog. For her the only escape is death. Her decision to take her child with her in death is, in a way, an affirmation of family ties, since she does not want Josie to be haunted, as she herself has been haunted, by the disappearance and abandonment of her mother. In the end, however, the play leaves audiences not only with a dead mother but also with a dead child—another in the assemblage of dead children whose fate suggests the difficulty with which Ireland is dealing with diversity and the steadily accelerating changes in what had been a remarkably stable homeland.

Inside or outside, the Midlands is ambiguous space, "a metaphor," as Carr herself put it, "for the crossroads between the worlds."[68] It is ideal if swampy—ideal in part *because* it is swampy—territory for exploring the ambiguity of human life and belonging. The Bog of Cats may lie geographically near the center of Ireland, but it represents above all marginal territory, a border area determinedly beyond the confines of "rational" control. As Melissa Sihra has pointed out, "specificity can constrict the work. Carr's landscape hovers between memory and imagination; between literary allusion and topographic realism."[69] Creating or re-creating that space on stage can be as challenging—and as wonderful—as the bog itself.

CHAPTER 4

Exploring Interiors

Frank McGuinness's *Gates of Gold* (2002)

Inhabited space transcends geometrical space.
—Gaston Bachelard, *The Poetics of Space*

Je suis l'espace où je suis.
—Noël Arnaud, in *The Poetics of Space*

Although Frank McGuinness is a significant Irish playwright with an international reputation, *Gates of Gold* (2002)[1] is not one of his best-known works. And although many McGuinness plays foreground recognizable portions of exterior Irish space, this one does not. Initially, then, a focus on *Gates of Gold* at the end of this study may seem counterintuitive. McGuinness's underappreciated play, however, provides an opportunity to examine stage space that contrasts with the spaces already considered while providing equally powerful nonverbal, nonlinear reinforcements of theme. *Gates of Gold* is set in a Dublin interior rather than in rural or exterior spaces of home and homeland. The restrictive space of that interior is surrounded by exterior realities full of challenges for same-sex couples, but focus remains on internal realities that are personal more than cultural—realities of love and partnership, life and death, and family. *Gates of Gold* shares the tendency of modernism and postmodernism to focus more on internal than external realities and to defy categories and binary opposites. By contrast with the other plays in this study, it illuminates what the term "Irish drama" implies, illustrating the reality that contemporary Irish lives are as often urban as rural, as often rooted in interior spaces as in exterior ones. *Gates of Gold* also destabilizes the dominant heterosexuality of Irish discourse and envisions a different homeland and additional ways of belonging to Ireland.

Both Marina Carr and Conor McPherson are younger than McGuinness. *Gates of Gold*, though, is the most recent play considered here, and McGuinness is as deeply rooted in the island of his birth as any Irish author. He has traveled widely and lived in both the Republic and Northern Ireland, but has never spent an extended time outside Ireland. He maintains close ties to the Donegal coast from which he comes but continues to live in the Dublin house he first rented as an undergraduate, resisting the self-exile of many of his characters (and of many other Irish authors). Of the authors considered here, only Brian Friel is as exclusively resident in Ireland (despite a 1963 sojourn in Minneapolis). Expressing sentiments worthy of Hester Swane in *By the Bog of Cats . . .* , McGuinness has maintained that he could not live outside Ireland: "It is impossible . . . I get physically sick when I am away for a long time."[2] Simultaneously, McGuinness has repeatedly noted, "I've always felt like a stranger. An outsider."[3] That tension between belonging and not belonging is a theme that has marked not only his comments about himself but also his plays.

Many of McGuinness's plays have a powerful sense of Irish geography and landscape. Though *Gates of Gold* is set in Ireland, however, and was inspired by the lives of two well-known Dublin residents, it depends on interior Irish space, in contrast to the exterior space foregrounded in the plays considered in other chapters. It places audiences in largely naturalistic urban interior space that is the site of the intimate lives of a same-sex couple. More specifically than the other plays considered in this study, *Gates of Gold* returns audiences to what Una Chaudhuri has termed modern drama's "favorite setting, the domestic interior."⁴ The use of urban space challenges the romantic and nationalistic notion that quintessential Irish space is rural space where peasants are rooted to the soil and free of the *gombeenism* that has kept much urban focus on money and profit. Furthermore, the set includes the couple's bedroom, typically the most private of spaces. By staking a claim to that private room, but doing so in the public space of a theater, the play establishes a space in which gay men can be seen and contests any lingering notions that they should be excluded from *any* space.⁵ The play tests traditional forms and assumptions, making what is strange familiar and implicitly demonstrating that the "Irish" story is not one but many.

The stage is divided into the more and less private areas of living room and bedroom—a physical separation as powerful as national boundaries, and equally important in separating "realms" and indicating power relationships. The identity of McGuinness's characters is tightly grounded in this interior space, which both protects and restricts them. Audiences allowed into these intimate lives must confront the implications of space and consider a specific instance of what Henri Lefebvre has delineated as the three contributors to our understanding of space: physical space, social space, and mental space. Lefebvre was seeking a unitary theory to make these spaces come together, but he also recognized the impossibility of either conflating or separating categories and emphasized that each "involves, underpins and presupposes the other."⁶ The physical space of McGuinness's urban home serves the needs of its residents, but excludes landscape so completely that it often seems closed and without context. Neither window nor dialogue allows glimpses of the surrounding physical space. It is inside space that matters.

One half of the bifurcated set is the living room of a residence occupied by Conrad and Gabriel, a couple inspired by Hilton Edwards and Micheál MacLíammóir, who in 1928 founded Dublin's Gate Theatre, where *Gates of Gold* would premiere almost eighty years later.⁷ The other half is the couple's bedroom, where the dying Gabriel continues to fret and strut. Like the set of Friel's *Philadelphia, Here I Come!* (1964),[8] this single naturalistic set presents public and private realms of interior space simultaneously and uses them to explore public and private aspects of character. Like the other plays discussed in this study, this one has action driven by the entrance of outsiders.

Csilla Bertha argues that "The famous cottage kitchen setting of many Revival plays and of their less original imitations . . . has been so much overused in Irish drama . . . that today, a playwright shows either laziness or great courage to set a play in a naturalistic house."[9] The peasant house that Bertha is discussing is literal and figurative miles from the urban house that constitutes the naturalistic set of McGuinness's play. An unstated referent to an archetypal cottage space likely to hold a place in an Irish audience's mental scrapbook of images, though, helps to establish the very different reality of *Gates of Gold*. It heightens audience awareness that the enclosed space of home holds the possibility of freedom as well as the clichéd reality of quarantine or incarceration. It also provides evidence that sophisticated, comfortable urban interiors, inhabited by artistic, well-read individuals for whom the text does not specify a regional dialect (though they use numerous Irish expressions), are nonetheless Irish. *Gates of Gold* presents an Ireland like the one Declan Hughes has identified as typical of his own work: "The Ireland that is the same as pretty much everywhere else in the world . . . What was important about Ireland . . . was what we had in common with other countries rather than what set us apart. The rural, the pastoral increasingly didn't seem to me to actually exist any more."[10]

The absence of regional Irish dialect fits the realities of Edwards and MacLíammóir as inspirations for Conrad and Gabriel, since it is generally believed that neither of the Gate founders was Irish. Born Alfred Willmore, MacLíammóir "translated" his name into Irish. Edwards abandoned the childhood name "Bobby" in favor of the more dignified "Hilton." Their consciously shaped identities parallel the performative aspects of gay life. Like the conflicting stories McGuinness's characters tell, these performative aspects test the credulity of others. The performances of Pyper in McGuinness's *Observe the Sons of Ulster* raise what Anthony Roche has described as the question of whether there is "a fixed sexual identity."[11] The performances in *Gates of Gold* raise the question of whether there is a fixed identity of any sort.

Edwards and MacLíammóir have, though, been widely and enthusiastically adopted by the Irish as important national figures. They belong to Ireland, despite the fact that sexuality like theirs was illegal and widely unaccepted culturally until the end of the twentieth century. Tributes to them abound; MacLíammóir's 1978 funeral was attended by an impressive array of political and religious dignitaries;[12] and the couple appear as background figures in several Irish novels. An irony both in the lives of these historical figures and in the lives of McGuinness's characters is that they belong, yet remain different. They belong and are at ease in their inside space, but indicate they have struggled in outside space, where they remain other. They are simultaneously of and outside Irish culture, just as their home is simultaneously part of and separate from the surrounding city.

The play's split stage has things in common with McGuinness's split stages in *Observe the Sons of Ulster Marching Towards the Somme* (1985) and *Mutabilitie* (1997), but these earlier plays are set in largely exterior spaces where characters establish often-shifting positions and realities without the benefit (or detriment) of restrictive man-made walls. A clearer parallel for *Gates of Gold* is Alan Ayckbourn's *Bedroom Farce* (1975), which McGuinness (who directed the play in 1983) has cited as an influence on the set of *Sons of Ulster*. The set of *Gates of Gold* gestures toward an entire tradition of sophisticated comedy more generally associated with the English than with the Irish: the set of Noel Coward's *Private Lives* (1929) can stand for that tradition.

The set also invites comparison with the use of space in Lorca's *The House of Bernarda Alba*, a play McGuinness directed in the late 1970s and adapted in 1991. The set for Lorca's play is the house of the title, which both defines and represents the reality of characters struggling simultaneously to preserve their own privacy and to break into the privacy of others. Like Nora's home in Ibsen's *A Doll's House*, which McGuinness adapted in 1996, Bernarda's home provides a naturalistic stage space that reveals the interior and exterior realities of the characters. McGuinness's stage space works in comparable ways, and, like Ibsen, he uses his title to provide a central metaphor with various levels of meaning. The Gate is the theater that the partners have founded and that becomes their legacy. The title also carries associations with metaphysical concerns and frames the play's consideration of Gabriel's looming death and of the men's love for each other.

The stage directions indicate that this space was purpose-built as a modern living space. It is, then, unlike the living space of Friel's *Translations*, which is filled with reminders of its earlier and alternate functions. The *Gates of Gold* set is also unlike the urban living spaces of Sean O'Casey's plays, which contain within them clear signs that they were not built as flats, but carved out of the more elegant homes of a previous era. On Friel's and O'Casey's sets, the tattered remnants of earlier realities signal changing spaces. But only the possibility that audiences remember the Irish stage's fondness for cottage space provides the home of *Gates of Gold* with signals of change; the space has no carry-over conventions from either cottage or tenement living.

The play's space is contemporary, and represents another indication of the difficulty of separating considerations of time and space. Certainly the play generally reflects the midcentury reality of Edwards and MacLíammóir, but inevitably it also reflects its early twenty-first-century production. McGuinness has identified the time frame of his play as "somewhere between 1982 and 2002,"[13] and the contemporary urban language influences audience reaction to the play's spaces.

Like *By the Bog of Cats* . . . this play resists the specific time signals so clear in *Translations* and *The Weir*. There is also less concern with avoiding the influence of English theater models such as those provided by Ayckbourn and Coward. References to Shakespeare enrich the play and fit the lives and experiences of the Gate Theatre founders, but references to the Masai, to poker playing in Las Vegas, to cocaine, and to the healing power of vitamin C seem more contemporary and establish a global context. Alma's singing of the Leonard Cohen/Jennifer Warnes "Song of Bernadette" (1986) is an anachronism in relation to the lives of Edwards and MacLíammóir, but meshes with references to the 1943 film *Song of Bernadette*. Audiences who know lyrics that do not appear in the script—"Torn by what we've done and can't undo / Just let me hold you"—will sense a direct applicability to the lives of these lovers.

O'Casey's flats and Synge's cottages provide their inhabitants with minimal privacy because they lack doors that may be locked. In *Gates of Gold*, Ryan's ability to enter at will may initially suggest an equal lack of privacy, but Ryan is a family member who may have a key, and Gabriel's description makes it clear that this home is a sanctuary of sorts for a couple that defies norms of the exterior world, where their sexuality makes them inherently outsiders: "For years being blackmailed was how we lived our lives . . . We could always expect a knock at the door or a letter . . . We were dangerous. We were men who loved each other and lived together openly as lovers when it was a fucking crime to do so" (51–52). Gabriel's use of "fucking" with its literal meaning is typical of McGuinness's often black and raunchy humor, while awareness that danger lies just outside the space of the set is a familiar McGuinness theme. In *The Factory Girls* and *Someone Who'll Watch Over Me*, to cite only the most obvious parallels, characters live under the threat of forces just offstage and out of sight.

Baudelaire's understanding that in a palace "there is no place for intimacy"[14] has long been shared by dramatists. Greek stages prompted a focus on largely public actions, and Shakespeare made extensive use of the Elizabethan stage's "inner" and "inner above" sections so that the placement of actors in smaller spaces would underscore the possibility of intimacy. On Greek and Elizabethan stages, then, there was an implication that the public world is the significant world. Stage space in *Gates of Gold* is crafted with places for intimate and more intimate scenes; public space is not a factor, despite the fact that these men have lived very public lives. It remains possible, however, to read this urban home as a continuation of the trope of home as nation, in which case McGuinness is providing a very different view of what the Irish homeland is or might become.

The living room has a couch and an armchair upholstered in red. It is "beautifully proportioned" and "sparsely furnished" (np). A large portrait of the couple in their youth dominates the wall, a visual reminder that the couple's past is relevant to their present—and that the youthful faces that first inspired love are not the faces of the present. For Joe Vanek's set in the premiere, the portrait was based on the 1937 painting *Medallion* by Gluck (Hannah Gluckstein).[15] *Medallion* presents Gluck and her lover in profile, one slightly behind the other, facing the same way, with short hair brushed off their foreheads and behind their ears. The youthful faces in the portrait contrast with the currently more mature faces of the characters, and audiences who recognized the Gluck connection were provided with a reference to another same-sex couple. The portrait's format also reflected the composition of a 1958 Gate Theatre memorial plaque that depicts Edwards and MacLíammóir in "rectangular bas-relief with their heads carved in profile."[16] Characters never refer to this representation of their youth and partnership, but periodically McGuinness's stage directions, like Tennessee Williams's in *The Glass Menagerie*, call for the portrait to get "intense" light (21) or to be specifically "illuminated" (62). Use of the portrait may also have been influenced by Ibsen's use of General Gabler's portrait in *Hedda Gabler* (1890), a play McGuinness adapted in 1994.

The text of *Gates of Gold* indicates that paintings of rural landscapes and seascapes are also on the living room walls. Unlike stage directions and dialogue in McPherson's *The Weir*, McGuinness's text gives no indication what landscapes are represented. It does, though, specify paintings, not photographs. Photographic images may in fact be no more "real" than paintings, but the use of paintings makes more obvious the intervention of artistic consciousness between reality and image. Characters never refer to the paintings. Lighting makes the joint portrait part of the play's discourse, but the link between the paintings and the play's action and characters is muted. It is also different in kind than the link between photographs and characters in *The Weir* that results from that play's extensive dialogue about the photographs. Paintings were not used in the premiere, perhaps because they would have overcrowded the relatively small set, but McGuinness's specification of them in the script indicates his awareness that the world of this play contrasts with Irish drama's ubiquitous use of rural spaces, which (had the paintings been used) would have been confined to literal frames rather than to the somewhat larger frames provided by the sets of Revivalist plays. Use of landscapes on the set would also have indicated that the inhabitants of this home, like the painters, were using their imaginations to inhabit the vast spaces represented in miniature by the paintings—illustrating a typical urban nostalgia for rural cultures untainted by crowds and busyness. Or, like the massive painting in McGuinness's *The Bird Sanctuary* (1994), they might have served to extend the reach of space beyond the space depicted on stage. Either way, the paintings would indicate a vicarious experience of landscape—the substitution of artistic images for direct experience of a natural world that the characters never mention and that they seem to have no interest in encountering directly. The intent of the text also seems to be that the paintings would be landscapes in the original definition of the word: "an artist's interpretation . . . of forms and colors and spaces . . . composed[d] . . . so that they make a work of art."[17]

The painting in *The Bird Sanctuary* provides an illuminating comparison. Eleanor has spent years painting the Booterstown Marsh, a transitional area between land and sea that is just outside her door but that she apparently never visits, though her nephew brings her specimens of weeds and water. McGuinness's stage directions specify that at the end of the play the back wall "melts" to reveal the bird sanctuary, and that the colors should be those already seen on stage, largely in spatters from Eleanor's painting. The feel of this conclusion resembles that of René Magritte's *La Condition Humaine* (1938). Magritte's painting presents a landscape painting propped on an easel before a window looking out on the landscape depicted in the painting. Painting and landscape merge to remind us of the difficulty of seeing anything without an individual and cultural frame.[18] A central irony in both Magritte's painting and *The Bird Sanctuary* is that in neither case are viewers seeing "reality." *Everything* in Magritte's painting is an artist's depiction, and though McGuinness specifies that the end of his play reveals the bird sanctuary (not Eleanor's painting of it), what appears is not the actual bird sanctuary but a depiction that picks up colors Eleanor has been using. Even if the set of *Gates of Gold* includes landscape paintings, the play retains a far more closed feel than *The Bird Sanctuary*, and outside space makes no real intrusion in either dialogue or image.

The living room dominated by the color red and the youthful portrait is balanced on the other side of the stage by the bedroom, furnished with a large brass bed covered in blue and a mirrored dressing table amply stocked with makeup that Gabriel uses to mask the signs of age. The text specifies that the sheets are white, which means they, like the wedding dresses in *By the Bog of Cats...*, will gather all available light. Sheets and mirror and brass bedstead will gleam even when the lights are dimmed.[19] McGuinness's meticulous detailing of a set with minimal complexity provides a visual focus on elements with key thematic import: the couple's portrait; Gabriel's vanity table; the bed. The power of these specific details would be dissipated if the set included common sickroom elements that more clearly indicated a time frame (television or computer) or that diverted focus from the ill person to the illness (bottles of medicine or a hospital bed).

At various moments in the play, lighting may illuminate one half of the set more completely than the other, but neither room ever disappears entirely from the audience's view. One result is to reveal the significance of silence and lack of motion, which here (as in *The Weir*) can be as powerful as dialogue and action: in Scene Four Alma sits in candlelight in the living room while Gabriel and Conrad talk in the bedroom; in Scene Six Gabriel lies asleep in the "near-darkened" bedroom while Conrad and Kassie play cards in the candlelit living room. Those juxtapositions, possible because the stage is split, interact with the dialogue to provide a nonverbal reinforcement of themes.

McGuinness's choice of terms—"living room" rather than "sitting room" or "parlor"—fits the play's less regional language and emphasizes the way stage space supports and reveals important themes. The "living" room is balanced by the bedroom, which might be termed the "dying" room.[20] Both areas involve incredible loneliness, emphasized by sight of a character alone in one room while the other room is populated. Connections between the spaces are evident not only because characters move from one to the other but also because, while Alma is teaching Gabriel how to die, he is teaching her how to live. Viewing the spaces simultaneously collapses them, thus collapsing the distance between public and private, life and death.

In the opening scene, Gabriel (alone in the bedroom) seems able to hear the living room conversation, and his words are regularly a response to what Conrad and Alma say. While production choices and actions could suggest they can hear Gabriel, there is nothing in the dialogue to suggest this. They do not seem to hear what Gabriel says, and audiences are free to interpret Gabriel's comments either as thoughts or as *sotto voce* remarks directed at himself (and the audience) rather than at Conrad and Alma. Later in the play dialogue in the two rooms overlaps, without implying that conversation going on in one room is audible in the other. The overlapping dialogue makes the script a challenge to read, but on stage (like similar moments in Eugene O'Neill's 1924 *Desire Under the Elms* and Tennessee Williams's 1947 *A Streetcar Named Desire*) it provides nuanced and reflective commentary facilitated by the split stage.

Other than the note that the stage is "bisected," a term that usually suggests an equal division, McGuinness's script provides no specifics about the size relationship of the two rooms. For the premiere, the stage space was a naturalistic box set equally divided between living room and bedroom. Imagining how differently the stage space would have operated had one room been larger and thus more prominent or important than the other reveals the significance of the equal division. The Gate Theatre for which McGuinness wrote the play has a relatively small proscenium arch stage that provided the premiere with space that reinforced important themes. The rooms were necessarily tight, confined spaces, and there was a clear separation between audience and stage. Produced on a thrust stage, or in the round, the play would have stage space that might well be larger and that would suggest a different relationship with the audience.

Size is only one indicator of space's role. An equally significant factor is how the space is used. In Samuel Beckett's *Quad* plays (1982), for example, four players are given precise paths to follow as they move around a square that is only six paces on each side. In *Quad I* the players move through the center of the square. In *Quad II*, though, Beckett outlines a pattern of movement that prevents any of the four from moving through the center of the square. The change from the pattern of *Quad I* to the pattern of *Quad II* alters perceptions of the space, particularly of the relationship of the center of the space to the four players.[21] In *Gates of Gold* the rooms are of equal size, but the important scenes take place in the bedroom, which gives primacy to the most personal, most intimate space.

The physical space of *Gates of Gold* presupposes a surrounding social space. As Lefebvre points out, the codes of space are established at specific periods of time and have their source in "the history of a people as well as in the history of each individual belonging to that people . . . new social relationships call for a new space, and vice versa."[22] Both sociological studies and literary portrayals often reveal an implicit assumption that queer spaces must be urban—the Left Bank, San Francisco, Greenwich Village, or the smaller urban areas of bathhouses, coffee shops, or city parks. In *The History of Sexuality*, Michel Foucault terms such spaces "places of tolerance."[23] Frequently, queer space is also perceived as nocturnal space. The typically urban and nocturnal world of theater has often provided a safe space for various sexualities. Actors and sexual minorities share an interest in performance. Performance is a trope for the probing of individual and cultural realities undertaken by many minorities. In this play it is actors and a same-sex couple who evince an awareness of the extent to which performative elements shape multiple aspects of human life.

Both the personal and the professional lives of this urban couple involve performative elements. Earlier McGuinness plays sometimes draw attention to metatheatrical moments. *Observe the Sons of Ulster* and *Someone Who'll Watch Over Me*, for example, have titles whose verbs suggest the basic role of an audience, and their opening dialogues may seem, at least in part, aimed directly at audiences. *Gates of Gold* opens with Gabriel before a mirror, applying makeup as though he were about to go on stage, and thus reminds us that plays and human behavior are both performances—the one perhaps no more real than the other.

The play's use of space, like its refusal to confine Conrad and Gabriel to a nocturnal world, requires clear shifts in assumptions. The play is a reminder of the difficulty Lefebvre identified in separating physical, social, and mental space—and another example of the ties between space and time. Same-sex desire in *Gates of Gold* is not sited in an appropriated urban space, used because the lovers do not belong in other spaces. It is instead sited in a conventional bedroom—space generally associated with desire—and there is an extent to which audiences are in (or out) of the closet, along with Conrad and Gabriel. The play's success in dealing with such issues openly is one indication of twenty-first-century shifts in Irish attitudes.

Whereas Irish drama (and Western drama in general) has traditionally presented both living room and bedroom as spaces in the homes of straight nuclear families, those spaces in *Gates of Gold* are the sites of a same-sex familial relationship not often represented on Irish stages. Rather than creating a new space for newly acknowledged relationships, McGuinness allows this couple to belong in familiar spaces. During the time he was working on *Gates of Gold*, McGuinness was adapting Strindberg's *Miss Julie*, a play that also focuses on "illicit" sexuality in an interior that is both protective and imprisoning and raises similar questions about who belongs in a home's various spaces. The sparring relationship of McGuinness's couple, alternately caustic and loving, resembles that of heterosexual couples in both *Miss Julie* and McGuinness's *There Came a Gypsy Riding* (2007). The play legitimizes discussion of same-sex love, calls attention to qualities shared by all personal relationships, and mounts an assault on conventional notions of public and private space that is as transformative as the emergence of various sexualities into the public space of parades and politics.

In "The Bed Space in Irish Drama," Joseph Smyth points to the creation of "bed spaces" in McGuinness's *Sons of Ulster* and *Carthaginians* (1988)—spaces created when characters spread out blankets to claim an area as "theirs."[24] These earlier plays (and 1982's *The Factory Girls*, which Smyth does not discuss) are particularly revealing when their bed spaces are juxtaposed to the bed in *Gates of Gold*. In the earlier plays, characters arguably had no proper bed spaces, and so they created such spaces by spreading out personal blankets in the very public spaces of an army camp, a graveyard, or a factory office. In *Gates of Gold* the characters have a bed—and a space for it—that is personal, private, and established in familiar ways, just as the bed space in Friel's *Philadelphia Here I Come!* is familiar. Whether the bed is regarded as a prop, a set piece, or simply as space, it is undeniably crucial space for the action of *Gates of Gold*. It is also a home space where the couple clearly belongs.

Earlier Irish plays like Geraldine Aron's *The Stanley Parkers* (1990) and Gerard Stembridge's *The Gay Detective* (1996) also include scenes in which male couples are in bed together. It is informative that neither play is mentioned in Smyth's discussion of bed spaces, which preserves a common notion of heteronormativity. McGuinness's couple is notable for their ordinariness: they have a long-term relationship; they do not have AIDS; Gabriel dies a natural death unconnected to his sexuality; though they are affected by social and legal biases against homosexuality, they seem not to live exclusively in shadows or fear. Though Gabriel might be described as a camping queer, Conrad cannot be relegated to that stereotype; together they indicate the varieties of individuals in same-sex relationships. And while there is much that is funny in this play, the humor does not denigrate the couple's relationship, which is treated with the same degree of seriousness accorded to heterosexual relationships. Men who love each other are not comic relief.

Imelda Foley describes the typical McGuinness setting as a "manufactured environment" in which characters are "removed from everyday society, in order that they may question and come to terms with social regimes which are mostly unidentifiable but govern their lives."[25] In factories, graveyards, army camps, and Mideast cells, McGuinness's characters form a "temporary alternative social order."[26] David Cregan persuasively links McGuinness's dramatic camp sites to "camp" as a queer aesthetic and to Foucault's identification of "heterotopias" that are simultaneously "outside all places" and "localizable."[27] Mirrors, like the one in which Gabriel is examining himself, Foucault describes as simultaneously utopias ("placeless" places) and heterotopias ("real" objects that exert a "counteraction," reminding the individuals reflected of their "absence" from the place where they stand and their "presence" in the virtual space of the mirror).[28]

Isolated in heterotopias ("real sites [that are] simultaneously represented, contested, and inverted"[29]), McGuinness's characters deliver litanies of place names: rivers in *Observe the Sons of Ulster Marching Towards the Somme* (1985), streets in *Carthaginians* (1988), towns in *The Bread Man* (1990), DART train stops in *Someone Who'll Watch Over Me* (1992). These litanies do not all function in precisely the same way. In *Carthaginians* and *The Bread Man* they expand the stage space by situating it in the larger geographic, highly politicized spaces of Derry and Donegal. In *Someone* they are reminders of a distant home, indications of what has been lost. In *Sons of Ulster* they both delineate what has been lost and mark the commonality of experience by linking Irish rivers to the Somme. Always, though, the litanies situate stage space in geographic space and conjure images of home, speaking of a naturalistic outside world that is not on stage and cannot literally be seen. Such references are missing from *Gates of Gold*.

The family in *Gates of Gold* is a microcosm of the larger world, where issues of life and death, loneliness, and the frequent conjunction of hurt, hostility, and love are also evident. The characters' direct references to the outside world, though, do not generally involve Irish place names. Gabriel's references to Irish laws and conventions about sexuality are specific to the island, and his reference to Alma as "herself alone" (18) is a variation on the common Irish slogan "Ourselves Alone." Places referred to by the characters, however, are not usually Irish places. These characters belong in the world at large, and there is a hint that they "overlook" Ireland just as Friel's Hugh "overlooks" England.

In another context, Nicholas Grene has examined how Irish stages often allow narrated, recollected, or recalled space to "invade the present, the represented space." The balance of "represented theatrical space" and "oral creation of alternative realities" that Grene analyzes[30] also operates in these earlier McGuinness plays, but less so in *Gates of Gold*. The play is clearly set in Ireland, though litanies of Irish place names are replaced by mentions of non-Irish geographic spaces (Salamanca, Peru, Kenya, Las Vegas, Argentina, Elsinore, and Wales, for example). Like references to portions of the British Empire in *Translations*, these establish a global context. The global references in *Gates of Gold* are of unreliable accuracy, but they indicate that Conrad and Gabriel, whose wanderings may be as theoretical as Hester's in *By the Bog of Cats*..., are searching for a home difficult to locate in Ireland. The two men create an Irish home, just as they create the theater they describe as their "child," but their stories indicate that they belong as much to the world as to Ireland.

Claire Gleitman's analysis of *Carthaginians* points to the "residual attractiveness" of the "notion of a cohesive Ireland attuned to a rich mythic past" and contrasts the nostalgia of Friel's plays with McGuinness's "determinedly postmodern attitude toward the land of his origin." Gleitman also notes McGuinness's "defiant stylistic shift away from the naturalism that has predominated on Irish stages."[31] Gleitman's comments about *Carthaginians* could also be applied to *Innocence* (1986), *Mary and Lizzie* (1989), and *Mutabilitie* (1997). By contrast, *Dolly West's Kitchen* (1999), *Gates of Gold*, and *There Came a Gypsy Riding* (2007)—all of which appeared after Gleitman's analysis—have clearly naturalistic sets and may surprise audiences who think they know this playwright based on the earlier works. The set of the opening production of *There Came a Gypsy Riding*, according to one reviewer, "owe[d] more to IKEA than to Synge,"[32] a comment that reveals clear assumptions about the norms of Irish drama. And the flights of fancy embodied in the spaces and lighting of some earlier McGuinness plays are almost exclusively confined to imaginative language in *Gates of Gold*—language that makes no effort to situate them in any of the culturally iconic rural areas of Ireland. There is no affection for Ireland's mythic past.

These characters have a home in the sense of a physical domicile, but the play also reminds us that they are often outsiders in an emotional sense, and that exile is part of the Irish experience and part of the human experience. Alma sings a verse from "Cutting the Corn Down in [Creeslough] Today," a song also known as

"Emigrant's Letter" and attributed to Percy French.[33] In the play's final scene, Gabriel sings (or recites, the script does not specify) lines from "Ballyhoe," by Eilish Boland.

> The whispers come, the whispers go,
> They each echo over the sea,
> A foreign land and a foreign strand
> Have taken you from me.
> Oh do you remember—remember—

The echoing whispers are like the whispers that have dogged this couple throughout their partnership. Gabriel is about to die, a final exile that will separate him from Conrad in ways parallel to the final separation exemplified by nineteenth-century emigration from Ireland. The finality of separation involved in that emigration was so clearly understood that the departure of relatives was "celebrated" with what the Irish called "American wakes," or "emigrant wakes." The emigrant songs in *Gates of Gold* echo that earlier Irish cultural experience and provide reminders that not all exiles are physical and not all involve the departure of the living. McGuinness has maintained that when his characters sing "they say what they mean."[34] Songs in this play provide an opportunity to consider the contemporary validity of traditional songs, to allow oral folk culture and modern (largely print) culture to interact, and to think about issues of home, away, and belonging in the context of Ireland's past and its present.

Many of McGuinness's earlier plays include strong reflections of Irish (particularly Northern Irish) situations, and in April 2002 (just as *Gates of Gold* was opening) he noted that the North "is there in everything I write, especially when it does not seem to be there."[35] Overt references to most Irish social and political conflicts are missing in this play, but concern with the legal and cultural position of Irish gays is a major focus, and since for McGuinness "the war in the heads, the war on the streets"[36] are regular parallels it is possible to make that connection in *Gates of Gold* as well. For audiences familiar with Edwards and MacLíammóir the play provides reminders of Dublin theater history, and those reminders enrich both the action and the dialogue. For audiences unfamiliar with the founders of the Gate Theatre, the play could seem to be set in any twenty-first-century urban part of the English-speaking world, and it demonstrates little concern with revisiting the tired question of what it means to be "Irish." It might, in fact, be seen as support for Declan Kiberd's recent contention that global economic realities have "put paid" to the very idea of a national literature.[37] Certainly the play puts paid to lingering notions of a conventional Stage Ireland. In *Gates of Gold*, fragmented references to places unanchored in verifiable plot elements serve primarily to disorient and may be seen as spatial metaphors that reflect the uncertain place inhabited by the play's characters, all of whom are outsiders in one sense or another and all of whom belong to Ireland. Conrad and Gabriel are simultaneously part of and separate from their Irish world, just as their home is simultaneously part of and separate from the surrounding city. They are Irish because they have chosen to be Irish and because they have made an Irish home where they belong.

Gaston Bachelard has pointed out that "all really inhabited space bears the essence of the notion of home,"[38] and despite their manufactured nature and the threats from offstage, spaces in the early McGuinness's dramas take on familiar essences of home. The manufactured places that characters inhabit are confining, but they are also protective. The relationship of visible onstage space to invisible offstage space is clearly revealed by dialogue. While threats also come from outside in *Gates of Gold*, the major threat is the inescapable biological reality of death. The protection afforded by Gabriel and Conrad's home is more comfortable than the manufactured spaces of McGuinness's earlier dramas, but their home cannot prevent the entrance of death, any more than the captives in *Someone Who'll Watch Over Me* could prevent the entrance of their captors.

The set for *Gates of Gold* has no visible surrounding exterior space of the sort commonly found on sets for Friel's plays or used in McGuinness's *Dolly West's Kitchen* (1999) and *There Came a Gypsy Riding* (2007). The absence of windows, of doors to additional rooms, and even of references to additional rooms is notable. The Harcourt Terrace house in which Edwards and MacLíammóir lived was large, with numerous rooms and windows, so McGuinness's choices are significant. The single door to the outside and the absence of exterior space or views suggests both that the world has rejected this couple and that they have rejected it. This possibly mutual exclusion heightens awareness both of the visible inclusions and of the invisible, excluded outside world. What is absent is as powerful as what is present. Bachelard's observation that "the imagination sympathizes with the being that inhabits the protected space"[39] undoubtedly fits the reaction to this play of most audience members. Just as readers instinctively sympathize with a first-person narrator unless something reorients their sympathy, audiences will instinctively "side" with Gabriel and Conrad, whose protected inside space seems familiar.

The high value that Western culture assigns to privacy has a complex relationship to same-sex couples. Regardless of whether interior and exterior space are coded feminine or masculine, couples who defy conventional definitions of feminine and masculine belong nowhere. Equally clearly, queer sexuality disrupts public space: expressions of same-sex affection remain forbidden, or at least unsettling, in much of the world's exterior spaces; and stereotypes inform us that gay male sex necessarily involves furtive encounters in the "private" space of public bathrooms or bathhouses. McGuinness's play, however, dismisses the notion that Conrad and Gabriel can be confined to spaces unwanted by straights and dismantles the notion that domestic space is exclusive to heterosexual couples. The outside world poses threats to Gabriel and Conrad that are as real as, if perhaps less extreme than, the outside threats in *Sons of Ulster* and *Someone Who'll Watch Over*

Me. Conrad's reference to worries about being "caged away" for a "crime against nature" (29) is a reminder of that. Home, however, has provided a measure of protection for the men. Seeing them in it, audiences are presented with a couple whose extraordinary professional lives and unusual ability to preserve love in the face of challenges highlight what they have in common with straight couples. Neither in public nor in private have Conrad and Gabriel been content with the metaphoric place to which society has relegated them. Instead, they have created their own quite literal places, and because an audience is present, this couple's private space has a very public dimension. Gabriel confronts Ryan (and thus the audience) with the fact that queers were hated and feared, in part, because their lack of visibility required others to "use their foul, fascinating imaginations," which made queers seem "dangerous" (52). *Gates of Gold* counters that invisible, imagined queer figure by making the lovers visible, familiar, domestic—dangerous only because they might threaten presumptions about the other.

This is not the first time that McGuinness, who makes no secret of his own long-term, same-sex partnership, has provided dramatic portraits that challenge lingering stereotypes about identity.[40] Most of his plays include characters who are either openly or by implication members of the gay/lesbian/bisexual community. The flamboyant Dido in *Carthaginians* and the powerful, often brutal Caravaggio in *Innocence* occasionally elicited strong audience reactions, in part because these plays disrupt and destabilize conventional space, reinventing it as space capable of accommodating diverse sexualities. Marco in *Dolly West's Kitchen* and Stephen in *The Bird Sanctuary* are less flamboyant and less outrageous. In these plays (as in *Gates of Gold*) the focus is more on normalizing understanding of diverse sexualities and creating a world comfortable with complexity and capable of recognizing common human realities. None of these plays is exclusively an effort either to queer conventional space or to normalize queer identity; it is always both. As a whole, McGuinness's dramas provide ample awareness of the complex, varied world of identity and belonging.

Just as Marina Carr's *By the Bog of Cats . . .* engages audiences in the literal and metaphoric spaces of a Traveller, *Gates of Gold* engages them in the literal and metaphoric spaces of a same-sex couple. Both plays present characters exiled from the Irish mainstream and examine the outsiders' efforts to come to terms with an established social regime and to create a home in Irish space. Empathy allows audiences "*to transcend the limits of [their] own world*,"[41] and enter imaginatively into the characters' world. Empathy may work in conjunction with a Brechtian cool rationality, but neither empathy nor logical analysis guarantees that audiences will modify their behavior once they leave the theater.

The sharpness of the division between the home's inside and the outside world in *Gates of Gold* is repeated by the sharpness of the division between living room and bedroom. In Gillian Rose's formulation, home is a "special place, to which one withdraws and from which one ventures forth."[42] This couple's bedroom is a particular place to which they have long withdrawn and to which Gabriel has now permanently withdrawn, though Conrad goes in and out. Intimate bedroom spaces are the most protected and hidden spaces in the Western world—spaces where individuals are free to be themselves, to reveal their most intimate realities. It is bedrooms that are most likely to be in our minds when we hope for the freedom of closed doors and the privacy of our own homes. Juxtaposing McGuinness's bedroom space to such earlier dramatic bedrooms as the one in *Philadelphia, Here I Come!* (where Gar can escape patriarchal patterns and enact his autonomy) and the one in *Juno and the Paycock* (which provides no refuge for Mary because it is not a separate room but is merely "partially concealed" by curtains) clarifies the set's impact. All three spaces are naturalistic and all three provide a modicum of protection. But only in *Gates of Gold* is the bedroom associated with actual (as opposed to dreamed-of) sex—albeit sex that the play does not depict.

Foucault notes that bedrooms separated from a house's other living spaces are linked not only to sexuality but also to the engendering of children.[43] Conrad and Gabriel are intensely aware of that link, and of the reality that they will never have children. Kassie suggests that she will "outlast" her brother because she has a child (32). Gabriel and Conrad compare founding their theater to conceiving a child (39), and Gabriel asks Conrad whether he regrets the fact they have no child (41). Conrad waffles in response, and in the closing scene Gabriel returns to the subject of the children who "were never born. All those *useless* nights in this *useless* bed." (64, emphasis added). Conception for them has meant the founding of a theater, which means it inevitably moved out of the privacy of the bedroom and into the public arena of the surrounding city. Work and conception have become not only one but also public, and audiences must accordingly reconfigure their associations with private space. For audiences who remember that the Gate occupies the Rotunda, once part of a Dublin maternity hospital, there are additional resonances.

Unlike the other plays in this study, and unlike multiple other plays by McGuinness, *Gates of Gold* has no dead child. Like the characters in these other plays, however, Conrad and Gabriel end in a state of childlessness. In that sense, all four plays present Ireland as a place with an uncertain future. By contrast, the family in this drama proves capable of nurturing. In *Gates of Gold* "family" includes blood relatives, a same-sex couple, and the nurse who arrives to help Gabriel die and learns, with his help, to live herself. It is a modern family, in tune with increasingly prevalent twenty-first-century values. It is also a realistic one, complete with cruelties, tensions, discord, and love. And it is a sustaining family, indicating that Ireland provides opportunities for establishing meaningful and supportive relationships that seem beyond the capacity of the family in *Translations* or the families in *By the Bog of Cats*. . . . As the "Song of Bernadette" has reminded us, the world is full not only of sorrows but also of mercy. To the extent that the play perpetuates the common Irish dramatic trope of home as symbolic of nation, *Gates of Gold* suggests a homeland capable of accommodating and nurturing a variety of individuals.

When the theater they founded takes the place of the child Conrad and Gabriel could not have, public conception replaces private conception and boundaries are blurred. Gabriel's opening actions in the bedroom suggest a similar blurring, but in the opposite direction. When the curtain rises, Gabriel is applying makeup before the bedroom mirror. He is also, it is later revealed, wearing a wig.[44] Ill and dying, he remains in the bedroom throughout. His absence from other space suggests his narrowing options. For him, there is literally no exit other than the final exile of death. His self-conscious adoption of the role of camping queer is the action of a vain actor, one aging and ill. It also brings elements of public performance into the private space of the bedroom and metatheatrical elements into the play. Gabriel's audience is small—Conrad, Alma, Kassie, and Ryan. For whom is he performing? Public actions have invaded this private space, and Gabriel has "escaped" into performance—just as Alfred Willmore escaped his identity by changing his name to Micheál MacLíammóir and adopting a new persona. When Gabriel literally throws away his wig, foregoing pretense and masquerade, his dramatic gesture indicates his acceptance of impending death and his acceptance of the role of private man in a private space.

Gabriel's deliberate self-creation also provides a visual image of the complexities of his marginalized identity. His personal and professional freedoms of expression are assertions of the freedom inherent in being an outsider, of not belonging to the mainstream. Discarding his wig is a rite of passage that could be seen as either a moment of self-discovery or an open acknowledgment of his aging reality. His situation is an example of what Joseph Allen Boone has described as the multiple levels of role-playing. Boone analyzes Joyce's use of a play format in the Circe section of *Ulysses* to portray an outsider (Bloom) whose sexual identity is complex, who looks in the mirror, and whose search for a child is a way of imagining the future. These are all themes and details that occur in McGuinness's play. Like the Circe section, *Gates of Gold* (which appeared after Boone's book was published) has sex that is "all linguistic."[45]

Audiences familiar with the Edwards/MacLíammóir partnership on which Conrad and Gabriel are based will inevitably feel this house shadowed by the theater that became the couple's lasting legacy. That was particularly true for the premiere, since it took place in that very theater. The script provides numerous hints of that external legacy, so that even audiences unfamiliar with the "real-world" prototypes of these characters will feel the offstage presence of their theater space. Conrad and Gabriel's conception of a theater and its company is part of their desire to turn "this town" into an Athens—or a Sodom (39), a reference that recalls the jest that Dublin audiences had a choice between Sodom (at the Gate Theatre run by Edwards and MacLíammóir) or Begorrah (at the nationalistic Abbey, with its early orientation toward peasant drama). The fact that this play, like McGuinness's *Innocence* (which was initially greeted with some public outrage), premiered at the Gate Theatre is a reminder that the founders' commitment to varied programming and inventive staging continues to be a significant legacy for Irish theatre.

The script specifies that in the play's final scene "The screen dividing living room and bedroom has disappeared" (62). If a production uses the disappearing screen, the metatheatrical moment works with the play's other performative moments to remind audiences that life inevitably involves a degree of performance. The disappearance might also suggest that divisions between these areas of greater and lesser privacy have dissolved. Like the back wall at the end of *The Bird Sanctuary* that "magically" disappears to meld the world of art and the world of nature, inside and outside, a disappearing screen in *Gates of Gold* could signal an end of divisions and boundaries. Or it might suggest merely that with the death of Gabriel there is no further need for the most intimate space.

The predictability and potential calm of this home reverse the unpredictability of the immense, unseen, exterior space whose dangers and opportunities are highlighted by the bedroom's confinement. The movement and development of audience identification with characters in *Gates of Gold* is almost completely opposite to the movement in earlier McGuinness plays with manufactured environments. In *The Factory Girls, Observe the Sons of Ulster, Carthaginians*, and *Someone Who'll Watch Over Me*, characters and their spaces initially seem less familiar, and audiences need time to understand the common human emotions and desires present on stage. In *Gates of Gold*, the curtain rises on a more familiar space of home, and audiences unfamiliar with the partnership of Edwards and MacLíammóir may realize only gradually that this familiar setting is home to domestic same-sex partners. Unlike most other art forms, dramatic performances take place in the same time as their reception: audiences cannot pause to consider the whole; they cannot flip backward to decide if anything has been missed or forward to determine whether they have correctly predicted developments. The point at which Conrad and Gabriel are recognized as a gay couple, then, depends on the knowledge and awareness that spectators bring to the performance. By the final curtain, though, the couple's relationship is undeniable.

McGuinness's use of prominent bed space allows for a gradual introduction to the intimacies of Gabriel and Conrad's relationship. The play is half over before the partners are seen together in the bedroom, and only in the play's last moments are they in bed together. When Gabriel's sister Kassie comes for a visit, Gabriel is sitting on a chair, and Alma is sitting on the bed. Kassie's presence in the bedroom is explainable because Gabriel is too ill to move to the living room. Her presence, however, is also the threatening penetration of an outsider into an intimate space where she does not belong. When Gabriel demands first that Kassie get off "the bed" and then that she get off "our bed" (31), his use of the plural pronoun reminds (or informs) the audience that he and Conrad have a sexual relationship. Kassie heightens the scene's sexual overtones by stretching out voluptuously on the bed, "using her fingers like claws" to disturb the bedclothes, and threatening to "creep into" the bed and "steal Conrad" after Gabriel's death (31–32). Bed space in Friel's *Philadelphia, Here I Come!* is individual, childhood space. That in Murphy's *Bailegangaire* is the individual space of an aging matriarch. In McGuinness's *Gates of Gold*, the bed space belongs to long-term sexual partners. McGuinness uses the space to present the couple's often mundane domestic realities, providing nonverbal reinforcements of major themes.

The space of this play is also mental space. Describing the contributions of humanists and feminists to the study of space, Gillian Rose has noted that "spaces are made meaningful through experience and interpretation, which makes [them] resonate with an extraordinary richness of emotion."[46] Rose's language directly parallels Seamus Heaney's description of the Irish as "inhabitants not just of a geographical country but of a country of the mind."[47] Gabriel and Conrad have produced their own space within the geometric confines of their home. It is a sheltered nest decorated to suit them and protected from a threatening outside. The rooms are mental space not because they are unreal or imagined but because this couple has created within them their own world—one that audiences can decode by noting not only what the space contains but also how it is used. Arguably, the limitation of pictures on the walls to a massive portrait of the lovers intensifies the reality that this mental space has become a sanctuary that excludes threats and others. Use of the landscapes called for in the script would lessen the sense that the exterior world is excluded. Gabriel's contention that his mother "never left the walls of our house after I was born" (9) may not be factually accurate, but it reinforces awareness of home as a place of intimacy, protecting inhabitants and excluding threats. Here, as in many McGuinness plays, Ibsen's influence is evident: the notion of home and the attention to wandering outside the home are informed by the Ibsen plays on which McGuinness has worked extensively.

Martin Heidegger's emphasis on the etymological connections of *dwell* and *peace* yields the conclusion that "*the fundamental character of dwelling is . . . sparing and preserving.*"[48] The dwelling established by Gabriel and Conrad transforms a space typically associated with heterosexual couples, just as the theater they established has transformed Dublin's theatrical world. The home's domestic space spares and preserves the couple from the perilous outside world.

The set's boundary between living room and bedroom establishes two different interiors, each with cultural and individual limitations. Like national boundaries or the sectarian boundaries of Northern Ireland, the clearly defined boundaries represented by walls and doors delineate areas with "rules" about who may enter and under what conditions. Room divisions in *Gates of Gold*, no less than the surveyor's boundaries being mapped in Brian Friel's *Translations*, mark restrictions about the crossing of boundaries and serve to divide "them" and "us." Just as mapped and thus organized space contrasts with the "disorder" surrounding it, just as Marina Carr's bog contrasts with the ordered space of a farm, the controlled and organized interior space of this couple's home contrasts with potentially dangerous disordered space outside. Bedrooms are the most restricted, most intimate of organized spaces. Initially, Kassie's son Ryan is not allowed into the bedroom of his uncle, much less onto the bed. He does not belong in the intimate space of the bedroom: his position as Gabriel's nephew does not counteract the offense of his past affair with Conrad. Ryan maintains that his father was blackmailed into marrying Kassie by her threat to name him and Gabriel as homosexuals, and Conrad seems also to have had an affair with Ryan's father. The tangled sexual relationships in this play include reminders that homosexuality was not decriminalized in the Irish Republic until 1993.[49]

Ryan does enter the bedroom later, challenging control over the bedroom space at a moment when Conrad is not present. Like his mother's earlier appearance in the bedroom, the scene feels like a home invasion, a private intrusion as significant as the intrusion of the British army into Irish space in *Translations,* or the arrival of an outsider in *The Weir,* or the crisscrossing intrusions into space in *By the Bog of Cats.* . . . Ryan's challenge to control of space is accompanied by a challenge to the medical authority represented by Alma, since he is also strewing oranges whose vitamin C he believes will save Gabriel. Ryan's penetration into the intimate space of the bedroom, a penetration parallel to the audience's penetration of private space, allows for a reconciliation of nephew and uncle. Just as this play (like all theater) confronts notions of inside-outside and onstage-offstage, it confronts ambiguities of restriction and openness, belonging and not belonging. Since, as Lefebvre points out, space is always socially produced, it is connected to power—to questions of "Who? . . . Why and how?"[50] Ryan sits on the bed but touches Gabriel only when he takes over shaving him. The use of bed space and touching constitutes visual communication that, even more than the dialogue, reveals the narrowing breach between family members.

With the exception of the disappearing screen and the occasionally expressionistic lighting, *Gates of Gold* features a naturalistic set and characters whose often fantastic rhetoric is accompanied by generally realistic behavior. McGuinness uses his naturalistic space to reveal not only personal, interior realities for these men but also wider social realities. The play closes with Gabriel and Conrad in bed together, kissing. It suggests, then, a widening possibility that all sexualities may be openly acknowledged and portrayed. It also reveals the inevitable pain associated with the exile of death.

Though Micheál MacLíammóir died in 1978, this play (which never mentions his name) is very much a twenty-first-century piece and relies on twenty-first-century notions of Irish space. The Ireland of this play is not only urban but also modern—a world of travel and hospice care and open consideration of sexuality. Ireland has joined the modern world, just as this couple has (in all but a legal sense) joined the conventional world of partnerships previously limited to heterosexuals. The play's language, generally free of regionalisms, contributes to the sense of modernity, and there is a conjunction of language and place. What is remarkable is neither Ireland's difference from the rest of the Western world nor this couple's difference from other couples.[51] The play's open consideration of this couple makes clear that Ireland has been incorporated into a modern Western (though not yet global) world that values pluralism, at least in its lip service. Edwards and MacLíammóir may have seemed an exotic couple early in the twentieth century, their sexuality overlooked in part because they belonged to the world of the theater.[52] McGuinness's play, though, suggests that modern Ireland is able to discuss sexuality and that this couple conforms to the domestic norms of contemporary Irish space. Ireland is now a space where individuals are able to define themselves less by resisting norms and more through embodying the new norm of inclusion. *Gates of Gold* also presents a space different than that of stereotypical rural Ireland, where iconic exterior spaces framed the lives of "ideal," chaste, submissive, self-sacrificing women (i.e., mothers) who had no erotic needs and were confined to a home in which sex existed solely for purposes of procreation. The Irish future has arrived, with neither priest nor colleen nor green fields in sight (though there are still alcoholics). Its space seems less "Irish," less concerned with modesty and chastity—and more global, more urbane, more progressive, more intellectual. It is a space where a wide variety of individuals may belong, and where "home" has a complex and flexible meaning.

Conclusion

> It is in the multiplicity of experience that we find the only possible meaning of our national identity and finally, too, the only possible value.
> —Garry Hynes, "Accepting the Fiction of Being 'National,'" *Irish Times*

In 1993, when she wrote those words, Garry Hynes was artistic director of the Abbey Theatre, a position from which she sought to broaden not only Irish theater's repertoire of "Irish" characters but also its conservative style, which rested too comfortably in the tradition of realistic theater. She was writing for the *Irish Times*, which suggests a felt need to engage a broad audience in consideration of why the national theater of an increasingly pluralist country ought to develop a flexible notion of what belongs on its stages. The plays considered in this study have not wandered very far from the representational, but they engage with multiplicities of Irish experience, representing various Irish sites on stage and using the stage space to reinforce themes.

The image of Ireland as a traditionally Catholic space, with nuclear heterosexual families, comfortable rural cottages, lilting accents, and green glens, persists both on the island itself and in the minds of potential tourists. The Irish, so stereotype has it, love their homeland. If they emigrate they long to return, a longing so intense it is passed genetically to children and grandchildren who have never been to the Ol' Sod. The Irish, the stereotype continues, celebrate their homeland in plays tied to national and political concerns, with broad popular appeal, so that taxi drivers and operators of B and Bs converse knowledgeably about what is playing at the Abbey. The plays considered in this study are traditional both in their awareness of that popular image of homeland and in their comfort with a generally realistic style. They exist within a continuity of Irish drama. Recognizing that continuity, however, risks oversimplifying the style of the plays as well as the ways in which they engage with images of the authors' Irish homeland. These plays interrogate traditional views and forms, questioning whether there is a fixed Irish identity and whether "Irish" itself might be a term devoid of set content.

The disproportionate contributions of Irish playwrights to world drama no doubt result both from their skillful use of the realistic tradition and from their ability to perpetuate what Nicholas Grene has described as "a separable category, fulfilling its own contrastive function in relation to the metropolitan mainstream." Grene argues that this contrastive function operates both abroad, where the plays are perceived as different because they are Irish, and at home, where the difference turns on "a gap in social milieu between characters and audiences."[1] The Irish settings and sets that are part of this tradition have broad appeal. In the plays examined here those settings and sets are not mere background but instead effective partners in communicating themes through nonverbal, nonlinear elements presented (among other ways) in the spaces of the set. It is the interplay of performance elements and textual elements that creates meaning.

Examining the plays together yields a renewed awareness of Artaud's insistence that theater *is* space and that the ways in which that space is filled matter greatly. The words and actions of these plays are crucial, but so are the Irish places represented on the stage spaces, and so is the determining influence of both actual places and stage spaces on characters and their actions. Audiences hear words and see movement; they envision the geographic places represented; they also see the stage space—and the picture the stage space provides shapes understandings of both Ireland and the Irish.

These plays share a firm relationship to specific Irish places, and they use stage space to create images and relationships that establish grounds on which audiences must perceive the action. The titles of three of the plays point to specific places.[2] These places existed before they became dramatic spaces, and they will continue to exist. They are also partially re-created by the impact of plays and productions, so that understandings of Irish geography shift. Travel lies in the background of all four plays, though the characters' identities are formed and grounded in Irish places. Healthy nuclear families are in scant supply, characters are white and Irish, children do not survive, death occasionally seems the only path to liberation. That mélange of change and continuity in the portrait of Ireland is paralleled by a mixture of change and continuity in the dramatic forms. These plays are innovative in many ways, but none ventures into extreme formal experimentation. They remain generally realistic, even when magic intrudes, and their use of space exists within the broad and flexible context of realistic theater.

It is easy to resist the temptation to reach global conclusions based on examination, however extensive, of four texts. On the other hand, juxtaposing the plays reminds us that though Ireland sometimes seems a small, homogeneous, traditional place, the island's specific locations vary tremendously in topography, in language and culture, and in the relationship of the characters to their slice of the homeland. Una Chaudhuri's examination of how the "massive and agonizing dislocations of the modern age . . . [are] making [their] voice heard in the theatrical language of the West"[3] provides a helpful angle from which to consider these Irish dramas, in which dislocations are felt not through homelessness or emigration or departure to new places but in the shifting understandings of the geography and culture of a traditional homeland. In these plays, Irish culture is increasingly disconnected from the history, knowledge, and love of geographical spots. Increasingly,

Irish drama both recognizes and appreciates the differences and complexities of characters who belong to this homeland.

In 1953 Eric Bentley observed that "the Irish were shamelessly exploited for centuries and they have shamelessly exploited the fact" particularly in their drama.[4] "Beneath the surface of [Irish] middle-class civilization there still lurked . . . a peasant culture possessing a living speech and not yet wholly robbed of simple human responses."[5] He also noted that "from the start the Abbey has been a theater of words, usually words spoken round a table" and complained that the Abbey storerooms contained only items suitable for "the naturalistic box-sets of Irish kitchens and living rooms."[6] In 1998 Fintan O'Toole emphasized a different aspect of Irish culture and drama: "Ireland had become an urban culture, plugged into the global economy, wired for the information age . . . people live out their lives suspended . . . between the real landscape they inhabit and the electronic images . . . that fill their screens . . . The plays might as well be set among . . . any culture that has lost its traditional bearings but not yet found a clear course."[7] Plays examined in this study span the decades between 1980 and the start of the twenty-first century. They illustrate the changes that fill the gap between the comments of Bentley and O'Toole, amply supporting the latter's contention that "'Irish' is an adjective that covers a multitude of differences."[8]

Like the playwrights, the characters in these dramas reside in Ireland, understanding their homeland not from the external perspective of foreign climes but from an internal, domestic perspective. Both playwrights and characters do, however, have perspective, whether they have benefited from world travel or not. They have the perspective of outsiders (Travellers or gays or urbanites in a rural world). They have the perspective of individuals watching their traditional worlds dissolve and reform because of invasion, urbanization, or globalization. They have the perspective imposed when outsiders arrive, forcing reevaluation of the meaning and importance of familiar places.

Conclusion • 131

Anthony Roche has pointed out the extent to which contemporary Irish drama has established dialogue as "central to the dramatic action," so that utterances can be called into question and disputed; the back and forth of storytelling, "verbal tennis," jokes, and arguments reveals all statements as provisional.[9] A similar doubleness is evident in the use of space by plays examined in this study. Local understanding of Ballybeg is challenged by the imposition of a map made by outsiders. Hester Swane's affection for the space of the bog is as powerful as the affection of Xavier Cassidy for his adjacent farm—yet fundamentally at odds with it. The pictures on the wall of Brendan's bar reveal varying relationships to the surrounding land that are as powerful as the contrasting stories characters tell. The confined space of Conrad and Gabriel's home and almost total exclusion of references to the surrounding city creates an implied contrast with what is missing; the contrasting spaces of living room and bedroom speak as powerfully as any segment of dialogue. These plays use space itself—the space of the stage and the spaces of Ireland—to expand a dialogue about home and homeland, belonging and not belonging, outsiders and insiders, self and others. When those spaces are examined in the multidisciplinary light of understandings developed by cultural and physical geographers, they can be seen as instances of the ways all humans react to space, and of the extent to which space is not merely a framing device but an indication that human and non-human spaces interact. As the Irish move further into the twenty-first century, understandings of their homeland will continue to evolve and to benefit from what is often a nonverbal dialogue (revealed through contrasting spaces and attitudes toward places) that accompanies what characters say.

Tracing the influence on Irish theater of Patrick Mason (artistic director of the Abbey Theatre from 1994 to 2000 and director of several Frank McGuinness plays, including *Gates of Gold*), Patrick Lonergan notes that for Mason the Abbey stage was "a symbolic space that allowed audiences to imagine new ways of being Irish."[10] Lonergan also notes that Irish theater understands itself better when it engages with non-Irish cultures and practices, and that engaging with the other allows a nation to "broaden and deepen its attitudes."[11] In these plays characters engage with one another, exploring and deepening their understanding of what it means to belong in Ireland—and allowing audiences to do the same.

In some ways the plays perpetuate the metaphor of family as nation, but these are families with a difference—nonnuclear families, "families" without blood ties, same-sex families, one-parent families, families with more than two parental figures. Fixed Irish identity is disrupted not only because families are no longer so clearly traditional but also because a more general locus of assured identity is disrupted. The Irish community is an expanding mosaic of families and individuals in tangled relationships with each other and troubled by tensions between belonging and not belonging. They exist in an evolving relationship with the physical spaces of their homeland. No longer exclusively agricultural, or even rural, Ireland emerges as a space of change. Residents seek a place, a home, in areas that are becoming part of a global world with changing relationships between people and space. Individuals emerging from a distinctive culture must negotiate new relationships with meaning and identity. There is no comfortable certainty.

Disruptions were created in nineteenth-century Ballybeg's understanding of place when outsiders arrived to map the area, implying that their modern instruments would enable them to master space. Disruptions continue as Ireland encounters and often welcomes the impact of far-reaching global and economic powers that change the physical and mental landscapes people inhabit. In Frank McGuinness's World War II play *Dolly West's Kitchen* (1999), Justin suggests that "If you're a Donegal man, you're true Irish," citing geologists who "discover what formations shaped a country like Ireland" and who have determined that the earliest formation was just off the coast of Donegal. His mother counters with an older understanding of Ireland that "everybody knows": "A little bit of heaven fell from out the skies one day, and when the angels found it, it looked so lovely there they sprinkled it with gold dust and they called it Ireland."[12] The "truth" of geologists challenges and is challenged by the "truth" of Rima's myth, just as the "truth" of the scientific instruments in *Translations* challenges and is challenged by the "truth" of local understandings of Donegal. Similarly divergent concepts of how best to understand Irish space and determine who is "true Irish" provide a connecting link for these and other Irish plays.

As multinational forces play out in an increasingly diverse Irish society, engagement with the other becomes both an inevitability and a source of new understandings. Engagement with the other includes engagement with the increasingly urban and suburban spaces that residents of the island call home. As Irish theater continues to engage with the geography and culture of its homeland, the ways in which various diversities are portrayed in stage spaces is worth further attention. Irish drama's places and spaces are not fixed but changing, responding to reconfigurations of home and homeland that will need new maps. "Always" is "a silly word."

Notes

Introduction

1. Eli Rozik, *Generating Theatre Meaning: A Theory and Methodology of Performance Analysis* (Brighton, UK: Sussex Academic Press, 2008), 91, 27. Italics in original.
2. J. L. Styan, "The Mystery of the Play Experience: Quince's Questions," in *Performing Texts*. Ed. Michael Issacharoff and Robin F. Jones (Philadelphia: U of Pennsylvania P, 1988), 9.
3. Seamus Deane, "Introduction," in *Selected Plays: Brian Friel* (Washington, DC: Catholic U of America P, 1984), 13.
4. Una Chaudhuri, *Staging Place: The Geography of Modern Drama* (Ann Arbor: U of Michigan P, 1995), xii. Italics in original.
5. The essays in *Performance and Place*, ed. Leslie Hill and Helen Paris (New York: Palgrave, 2006) also offer interesting perspectives.
6. T. S. Eliot, "The Possibility of a Poetic Drama," in *The Sacred Wood: Essays on Poetry and Criticism* (1922). http://www.bartleby.com/200/sw5.html (accessed August 24, 2009).
7. T. S. Eliot, "Poetry and Drama" (1951), in *On Poetry and Poets* (New York: Noonday, 1961), 75–95.
8. Quoted in Eileen Battersby, "Marina of the Midlands," *Irish Times*, May 4, 2000, 15.
9. See Julia A. Walker, "The Text/Performance Split across the Analytic/Continental Divide," in *Staging Philosophy: Intersections of Theory, Performance and Philosophy*, ed. David Krasner and David Z. Saltz (Ann Arbor: Michigan UP, 2006), 36.
10. Erika Fischer-Lichte, "Theater as a Cultural System," in *The Semiotics of Theater*, trans. Jeremy Gaines (Bloomington: Indiana UP, 1992), 15.
11. Richard Hornby, *Script into Performance: A Structuralist Approach* (New York: Paragon House, 1987), ix.
12. Gay McAuley, *Space in Performance: Making Meaning in the Theatre* (Ann Arbor: Michigan UP, 1999), 17.

13. See Henri Lefebvre, *The Production of Space* (1974), trans. Donald Nicholson-Smith (Oxford UK: Blackwell, 1991), and Matthew Johnson, *An Archaeology of Capitalism* (Oxford, UK: Blackwell, 1996), for complete discussions of the intersection of physical and mental shapes.
14. Michael Issacharoff distinguishes between "didascalia" (comments in the authorial voice) and "glossing comments" in dialogue. "Stage Codes," in *Performing Texts*, ed. Issacharoff and Robin F. Jones (Philadelphia: U of Pennsylvania P, 1988), 62. Eli Rozik makes a somewhat parallel distinction between "directive" and "descriptive" speech in *Generating Theatre Meaning*, 56.
15. Gerry Smyth, *Space and the Irish Cultural Imagination* (New York: Palgrave, 2001), and Liam Harte, Yvonne Whelan, and Patrick Crotty, eds., *Ireland: Space, Text, Time* (Dublin: Liffey Press, 2005).
16. Victor Turner, "Passages, Margins, and Poverty: Religious Symbols of Communitas" (1972), in *Dramas, Fields, and Metaphors: Symbolic Action in Human Society* (Ithaca: Cornell UP, 1974), 231–70.
17. Nicholas Grene, *The Politics of Irish Drama: Plays in Context from Boucicault to Friel* (Cambridge, UK: Cambridge UP, 1999), 264.
18. Patrick Lonergan, *Theatre and Globalization: Irish Drama in the Celtic Tiger Era* (New York: Palgrave Macmillan, 2010), 91.
19. Seamus Heaney, "Place and Displacement: Recent Poetry from Northern Ireland" (1984), in *Finders Keepers: Selected Prose 1971–2001* (New York: Farrer Straus, 2002), 126.
20. Ibid., 125.
21. Declan Hughes, "Who the Hell Do We Think We Still Are? Reflections on Irish Theatre and Identity," in *Theatre Stuff: Critical Essays on Contemporary Irish Theatre*. ed. Eamonn Jordan (Dublin: Carysfort Press, 2000), 8, 13.
22. Eamonn Jordan, "Urban Drama: Any Myth Will Do?" in *The Dreaming Body: Contemporary Irish Theatre,* ed. Melissa Sihra and Paul Murphy (Gerrards Cross, UK: Colin Smythe, 2009), 25.
23. A useful introduction to such issues is Marvin Carlson, *Places of Performance: The Semiotics of Theatre Architecture* (Ithaca, NY: Cornell UP, 1989).
24. Derry City (known to the Unionist community as Londonderry) is a border town that has often been a flash point for Irish troubles. Derry's Guildhall is the seat of the city's government. It has been attacked more than once by terrorists, and it was the site of hearings into the events of Ireland's 1972 Bloody Sunday. Even when the first production of *Translations* toured, its premiere in the Guildhall was generally a subject of comment.
25. James Joyce, *A Portrait of the Artist as a Young Man* (1916) (New York: Bedford/St. Martin's, 1993), 218.

Chapter 1

1. It is also worth remembering Dromio in *The Comedy of Errors* (c. 1589), who describes the maid as a globe with Ireland represented by her buttocks, and Spenser's *A View of the Present State of Ireland* (1596), in which Eudoxus produces a map that he says will guide understanding of Ireland. The impact of Spenser's *View* on Irish literature is hard to overestimate. For another instance of its relevance to contemporary Irish drama, see Frank McGuinness's *Mutabilitie* (1997), in which Spenser is a character and in which characters in Act Three echo the dialogue of Eudoxus and Irenius in *View*.
2. Brian Friel, *Translations* (London: Faber and Faber, 1981), 51, 52, 53. Emphasis added. All references are to this edition and are cited in parentheses.
3. Brian Friel, "Extracts from a Sporadic Diary (1979): *Translations*," in *Brian Friel: Essays, Diaries, Interviews: 1964–1999*, ed. Christopher Murray (New York: Faber, 1999), 75.
4. Friel has repeatedly expressed admiration for Chekhov and has adapted four of his plays (all of them after *Translations*). For a full discussion of Chekhov's mutating sets, see Hanna Scolnicov, "Preferring Insecurity," in *Woman's Theatrical Space* (Cambridge, UK: Cambridge UP, 1994), 109–125.
5. Stiofán Ó Cadhla, *Civilizing Ireland: Ordnance Survey 1824–1842: Ethnography, Cartography, Translation* (Dublin: Irish Academic Press, 2007), 13. Ó Cadhla notes that "there has never been a comprehensive official cartography of the island of Ireland . . . in the Irish language" and points out that an early Irish term for *map* (*mapa*) was a transliteration of the English, and that the more recent term, *léirscáil*, is a recent neologism. See also William J. Smyth, *Map-Making, Landscapes and Memory: A Geography of Colonial and Early Modern Ireland c. 1530–1750* (Cork: Cork UP, 2006).
6. See, for example, Helen Lojek, "Brian Friel's Plays and George Steiner's Linguistics: Translating the Irish," *Contemporary Literature* 35 (Spring 1994): 83–99. Reprinted in *Contemporary Literary Criticism*, 115: 239–45.
7. William Yolland, an English officer Andrews describes as "of outstanding scientific ability," wrote the official account of the Loch Foyle base that was part of the Ordnance Survey. T. F. Lancey worked with the survey in either the 1820s or the 1830s, and a Lieutenant Lancey (W. Lancey) was working in Donegal with the survey. See J. H. Andrews, *A Paper Landscape: The Ordnance Survey in Nineteenth-Century Ireland* (1975) (Dublin: Four Courts, 2002), 50–52 and 151–52. Ó Cadhla's study and Gillian M. Doherty's *The Irish Ordnance Survey: History, Culture and Memory* (Dublin: Four Courts Press, 2004) are also of interest, though they did not influence Friel.
8. In the 1830s a series of parish histories, known as the Ordnance Survey Memoirs, were begun, aimed at preserving what Andrews terms the "historical geography of pre-famine Ireland" (149): cultural information (about religious, folk, and social patterns) and facts (about Irish history, economics, and flora/fauna).

Only accounts of the northern parishes were completed before the scheme was abandoned, and a single account was published at the time. In the 1990s, well after Friel was writing, the Institute of Irish Studies at Queen's University Belfast published all 40 of the completed memoirs, under the editorship of Angélique Day and Patrick McWilliams.

9. Declan Kiberd, *Inventing Ireland: The Literature of the Modern Nation* (London: Jonathan Cape, 1995), 620.
10. These distinctive ways of seeing landscape are detailed by John Brinckerhoff Jackson, *Discovering the Vernacular Landscape* (New Haven: Yale UP, 1984), x–xi. Jackson distinguishes between seeing landscape "as a phenomenon, a space or collection of spaces" and seeing it "as the setting of certain human activities" or seeing "the history of the landscape itself, how it was formed, how it has changed, and who it was who changed it."
11. Gerry Smyth, *Space and the Irish Cultural Imagination* (New York: Palgrave, 2001), 19–20. Smyth is building on ideas explored earlier by Raymond Williams in *Problems in Materialism and Culture: Selected Essays* (London: Verso, 1980).
12. Bernard Klein, *Maps and the Writing of Space in Early Modern England and Ireland* (New York: Palgrave, 2001), 63.
13. Ibid., 184.
14. Quoted in Klein, *Maps*, 209.
15. Including that in Friel's *Philadelphia, Here I Come!* (1964), in which Madge serves as a surrogate mother.
16. British "kitchen sink" drama of the 1950s and 1960s is similar to Irish cottage kitchen drama in its emphasis on local dialects, interior sets, and sympathy with the poor. It, too, can be seen as antiestablishment, but the urban focus and frequent anger give it a very different feel.
17. From an early draft of Henry's *An Irish Portrait* (1951), quoted in S. B. Kennedy, *Paul Henry* (New Haven: Yale UP, 2007), 84. Henry's approach was controversial, even at the time, ranging from praise of his evocation of "the true Ireland" (Kennedy, 68) to questions about whether his paintings "represent modern Ireland as it is to-day or [are] merely a product of fancy, the sort of fancy that was prevalent here twenty years ago" (Kennedy, 79). Henry painted into the 1940s, but his work remains overwhelmingly focused on the rural western landscapes to which he fled, despite his roots in Belfast and his ties to Dublin. Two less rural pieces—*The Custom House, Dublin* (1929) and *The Harbour, Balbriggan* (1935–40)—were both commissioned, and his relatively few Belfast paintings typically depict the cityscape from a distance, so that it merges with the landscape.
18. Seamus Heaney, "The Sense of Place," in *Preoccupations: Selected Prose 1968–1978* (London: Faber and Faber, 1980), 136.
19. Patrick Duffy has linked the Irish "preoccupation with rural imagery" to "nineteenth-century searches for an identity as Other to English industrial

urbanism." "Writing Ireland: Literature and Art in the Representation of Irish Place," in *In Search of Ireland: A Cultural Geography*, ed. Brian Graham (London: Routledge, 1997), 69.
20. Edward Hirsch, "The Imaginary Irish Peasant," *PMLA* 106:5 (October 1991): 1116–33.
21. J. M. Synge, Preface to *The Playboy of the Western World* (1907) in *The Complete Plays* (Oxford: Oxford University Press,1995), 96–97.
22. Similarly, in Friel's *The Gentle Island* (1971) residents of the western island reject the romantic image that so enchants Peter, a visitor. Both *The Gentle Island* and *Translations* are situated in moments of huge cultural change. Michael Parker notes that Friel's "decoding" of de Valera's dream of romantic, rural Ireland is close to Seán O'Faoláin's take on that "romantic illusion." "Telling Tales: Narratives of Politics and Sexuality in *The Gentle Island*," in *Brian Friel's Dramatic Artistry: 'The Work Has Value,'* eds. Donald Morse, Csilla Bertha, and Mária Kurdi (Dublin: Carysfort Press, 2006), 153.
23. P. J. Dowling, *The Hedge Schools of Ireland* (1935) (Cork: Mercier Press, 1968). Hugh is also similar to the portrait provided in the other best-known depiction of hedge schools, William Carleton's "The Hedge School," in *Traits and Stories of the Irish Peasantry* (1842–44). Project Gutenberg EBook #16014 (accessed September 2008). Carleton, who attended a hedge school in County Monagham from 1814 to 1816, described the "inordinate love of whisky" and "slight touch of derangement" (4) that frequently characterized hedge school masters, who were commonly "unfeeling tyrants" (29). His outline of common hedge school curricula includes spelling, math, geography, and classics in both Latin and Greek, but is more varied that the curriculum Hugh imposes. Carleton's master, like Hugh, leaves class to go for a drink, and speaks to his students in a mixture of English and Latin (29). Carleton also describes "a lame young man" who serves as a hedge schoolmaster. Antonia McManus, in *The Irish Hedge School and Its Books, 1695–1831* (Dublin: Four Courts, 2002), 118, quotes Padraic Colum's poetic recollection:

> My eyelids red and heavy are
> With bending o'er the smould'ring peat
> I know the Aeneid now by heart
> My Virgil read in cold and heat.

24. When Maire quotes Daniel O'Connell's opinion that the "old language" (Irish) is "a barrier to modern progress" (28), she gives the same Benthamite argument a positive twist. She is also accurately repeating the argument of O'Connell, who declared himself "sufficiently utilitarian not to regret" the abandonment of Irish. See McManus, *The Irish Hedge School*, 131.

25. Heaney, "Sense of Place," 131. Heaney served with Friel on the board of Field Day Theatre Company, which first produced *Translations*. He has a body of place-name (and other) poems that consider issues parallel to those in *Translations*.
26. Matthew Johnson, *An Archaeology of Capitalism* (Oxford, UK: Blackwell, 1996), 90, 72, 114–15.
27. Simon Schama, *Landscape and Memory* (New York: Knopf, 1995), 10.
28. European Landscape Convention, Chapter I, Article I. (Adopted 2000; in force 2004.) http://www.coe.int/t/dg4/cultureheritage/heritage/Landscape/default_en.asp (accessed March 10, 2010).
29. Frank McGuinness makes the same connection in *Mutabilitie* (London: Faber, 1997).
30. Andrews, *Paper Landscape*, 124.
31. Ibid., 120, 119, 120.
32. When Bridget pays Hugh, for example, the sums she mentions (26) are less than those reported by Dowling (82), but she matches Dowling's account in indicating that charges for math instruction are greater than those for instruction in writing.
33. McManus, in *The Irish Hedge School,* reports that "the absence of a wide variety of printed books in [Irish]" made the task of hedge schoolmasters who wished to teach Irish "much more difficult," 132. The general question of what books might have been used in hedge schools is complex. Under Queen Elizabeth I, the Bible was translated into Irish as part of the English effort to circumvent the influence of Catholic priests and encourage adherence to reformed religion, yet Irish language books remained rare and expensive. Authors of nineteenth-century English language readers "felt no need to inform their readers of life beyond the rural scene," and there was little vocational training. Once the national school system was established, however, control over texts tightened and the focus of materials changed. The *Fourteenth report of the commission of the Board of Education in Ireland* (1812–13) complained that books used in hedge schools were "calculated to incite lawless and profligate adventure, to cherish superstition, or to lead to dissention or disloyalty" and disapproved of using works like *Tristram Shandy* and *The Monk*. Under the Board of Education, books on spelling, arithmetic, and geography were produced, and new texts, while they took a more secular approach, were permeated by Christian ethics and marginalized the non-Christian civilizations of Greece and Rome. See J. M. Goldstrom, *The Social Content of Education: 1808–1870: A Study of the Working Class School Reader in England and Ireland* (Shannon: Irish UP, 1972), 26, 55–56, 78, 68–69. In broad outline, then, Hugh's practices follow those that historians cite as typical of Irish hedge schools: there is no vocational education, the anti-English bias is evident, and questioning remains the dominant pedagogical technique. Hugh's emphasis on Virgil not only allows for avoidance of the Irish-English

language issue but also provides an opportunity for him to demonstrate an anti-English bias.
34. Nicholas Entrikin, *The Betweenness of Place: Toward a Geography of Modernity* (Baltimore: Johns Hopkins UP: 1991), 2.
35. Chris Murray points out that after the 1829 Catholic Emancipation Act hedge schools were no longer illegal. Establishment of the National Education Board, then, meant that hedge schools "became redundant as soon as they were legal." "Palimpsest: Two Languages as One in *Translations*," in *Brian Friel's Dramatic Artistry: "The Work Has Value,"* ed. Donald E. Morse, Csilla Bertha, and Mária Kurdi (Dublin: Carysfort, 2006), 97.
36. Vivian Mercier, discussing Irish satire in the eighteenth century, when the Irish were losing both country and language, has noted that "their language [Irish], like the culture it represented, was still a protecting hedge from behind which they could snipe at the English; but there must have been small satisfaction in launching an attack whose essential condition was that the enemy should never become aware of it." *The Irish Comic Tradition* (Oxford, UK: Clarendon, 1962), 171. Manus's use of Irish is also a form of sniping, and his satisfaction, too, must have been small.
37. References to Beckett's rejoinder appear frequently in Irish Studies, generally without specific documentation. Seamus Heaney endorsed Beckett's comment in a 1981 interview. Frank Kinahan, "Artists on Art: An Interview with Seamus Heaney," in *Critical Inquiry* 8 (Spring 1982): 407. Roy Foster included it in *Heathcliff and the Great Hunger: Studies in Irish Culture* (London: Verso, 1995), 127. Tom Paulin used the line in his poem "On Being Dealt the Anti-Semitic Card," in the *Guardian*, January 8, 2003, http://www.guardian.co.uk/education/2003/jan/08/internationaleducationnews.higher education (accessed May 2011). And Roy Foster used the story again in "Say It Again, Sam," in the *London Sunday Times*, March 11, 2009, http://entertainment.timesonline.co.uk/tol/arts_and_entertainment/books/article7393111.ece (accessed May 2011).
38. Henri Lefebvre, *The Production of Space* (1974), trans. Donald Nicholson-Smith (Oxford, UK: Blackwell, 1991), 1–2.
39. Declan Kiberd, *Inventing Ireland: The Literature of the Modern Nation* (London: Vintage, 1996), 620.
40. Patrick Lonergan, *Theatre and Globalization: Irish Drama in the Celtic Tiger Era* (New York: Palgrave Macmillan, 2010).
41. Carleton, 31. See also McManus, *Irish Hedge School*, 36.
42. The later parallel difficulties of communication between Yolland and Maire are warmly and touchingly humorous, more than parodic.
43. The report is reprinted in an appendix to Andrews's *A Paper Landscape*. Andrews' report of debates about the appropriate scale of the maps is the sort of British historical reality Lewis Carroll was satirizing when a character reports that, having expanded their maps to a "scale of *a mile to the mile!*,"

people abandoned the entire mapmaking enterprise: "we now use the country itself, as its own map, and I assure you it does nearly as well." "The Man in the Moon" in *Sylvie and Bruno Concluded* (1893), in *The Complete Sylvie and Bruno* (San Francisco: Mercury House, 1991), 265. I am grateful to Robert Tracy for pointing me in the direction of a similar piece by Jorge Luis Borges: "On Exactitude in Science," in *A Universal History of Infamy*, trans. Norman Thomas di Giovanni (New York: Penguin, 1975).

44. For a feminist discussion of similar issues, see Catherine Nash, "Remapping and Renaming: New Cartographies of Identity, Gender and Landscape in Ireland," in *Feminist Review* 44 (Summer 1993), 39–57. And see Nash's "Reclaiming Vision: Looking at Landscape and the Body," in *Gender, Place and Culture: A Journal of Feminist Geography* 3, no. 2 (1996): 149–70.

45. Friel's awareness of the power of set pieces and the arrangement of stage space is also evident in the opening scene of *Wonderful Tennessee* (1993), when, for long moments before the characters enter, audiences see stage space centered by a wooden stand, "cruciform in shape, on which hangs the remnant of a life belt." The shape mimics that of the well-known Celtic high cross, which has a ring at the intersection of the cross's arms. Attention is focused on a tattered reminder of a faith missing from the lives of the characters and contrasted with other references to faith. I have discussed stage space in *Wonderful Tennessee* more completely in "Space in *Wonderful Tennessee*," in *Irish Theatre International* 2, no. 2 (August 2009): 48–61.

46. Garrett A. Sullivan, Jr., *The Drama of Landscape: Land, Property, and Social Relations on the Early Modern Stage* (Stanford: Stanford UP, 1998), 108.

47. Terence Hawkes, *Meaning by Shakespeare* (London: Routledge, 1992), 121.

Chapter 2

1. Conor McPherson, "If you're a young Irish playwright, come to London . . . ," *New Statesman* 11, no. 492 (February 20, 1998): 40.
2. Conor McPherson, "Late Nights and Proclamations: The playwright recounts the beginnings of *The Weir*," *American Theatre* (April 1999): 45.
3. Conor McPherson, *The Weir* (London: Nick Hern, 1998), 1. Subsequent references are to this edition and are incorporated in the text.
4. McPherson, "Late Nights," 45.
5. Demands on the actors, though, might allow them to approximate the Abbey style. Max Beerbohm reported observing Abbey actors rehearsing on a miniscule stage with the "conscious inexpressiveness" of "blank faces and stiff movements." Quoted in James Flannery, "W. B. Yeats and the Abbey Theatre Company," in *Educational Theatre Journal* 27, no. 2 (May 1975): 190.
6. Quoted in McPherson, "If you're a young Irish playwright," 40.

7. From an early draft of Henry's *An Irish Portrait* (1951), quoted in S. B. Kennedy, *Paul Henry* (New Haven: Yale UP, 2007), 84. See note 10 in Chapter One of this study.
8. See www.irishtourist.com (accessed April 8, 2007).
9. This conventional urban-rural, utilitarian-romantic distinction, of course, parallels the long tradition of distinguishing Ireland from England on the basis of its more rural, less commercial, more romantic culture.
10. Eamonn Jordan, *Dissident Dramaturgies* (Dublin: Irish Academic Press, 2010), 116.
11. A traditional Irish distinction between "bar" as male space and adjacent "lounge" as female space does not seem to apply here, since there is only one space. "Bar," then, seems more contemporary than "pub."
12. Patrick Duffy, *Exploring the History and Heritage of Irish Landscapes* (Dublin: Four Courts Press, 2007), 151, 153.
13. Susan Sontag, *On Photography* (New York: Farrar, Straus and Giroux, 1977), 10.
14. Simon Schama, *Landscape and Memory* (New York: Knopf, 1995), 12.
15. In Brian Friel's *Wonderful Tennessee*, a character's failure to photograph dolphins casts doubt on his claim to have seen them. Only a photo would prove them real.
16. Conor McPherson, "Author's Note" in *This Lime Tree Bower: Three Plays* (Dublin: New Island Books, 1996), np. Emphasis in original.
17. Seamus Deane, "The Production of Cultural Space in Irish Writing," in *boundary* 221, no. 3 (1994): 130.
18. Ibid.,117–44.
19. S. B. Kennedy, *Irish Art and Modernism: 1880–1950* (Belfast: Institute of Irish Studies, 1991), 180.
20. Fintan Cullen, *Visual Politics: The Representation of Ireland 1750–1930* (Cork: Cork UP, 1997), 168–69.
21. Fáilte Ireland and The Heritage Council, *Climate Change, Heritage and Tourism: Implications for Ireland's Coast and Inland Waterways: Summary Document* (Dublin: The Heritage Council of Ireland Series, 2009), 42.
22. John Cashman, *Probing the Past for the Present: The Northern Irish Border. Character and Community* (Bloomington: Indiana UP, 2009).
23. John Wilson Foster, "Nature and Nation in the Nineteenth Century," in *Nature in Ireland: A Scientific and Cultural History*, ed. John Wilson Foster (Dublin: Lilliput, 1987), 412–13.
24. John Montague, *The Rough Field* (Newcastle upon Tyne: Bloodaxe, 1990).

> The whole landscape a manuscript
> We had lost the skill to read,
> A part of our past disinherited (1972)

25. See Ona Frawley, *Irish Pastoral: Nostalgia and Twentieth-Century Irish Literature* (Dublin: Irish Academic Press, 2005), 44. Frawley quotes Malcolm Andrews,

The Picturesque (Helm Information Literary Sources and Documents Series, 1994).
26. "So there's these three Irishmen." Interview with Tim Adams. *The Sunday Observer* (February 4, 2001); and "An Interview with Conor McPherson," http://www.thelowry.com/shows/seafarer.html (accessed 8 April 2007).
27. Martin McDonogh's plays make for an interesting comparison.
28. Quoted in Declan Kiberd, *The Irish Writer and the World* (Cambridge, UK: Cambridge UP, 2005), 40.
29. William Wordsworth, "Lines: Composed a Few Miles above Tintern Abbey" (1798), in *The Poetical Works of William Wordsworth*, ed. E. de Selincourt (Oxford: Clarendon Press, 1944), 262.
30. Quoted in Mel Gussow, "From Dublin to Broadway, Spinning Tales of Irish Wool," *New York Times,* April 1, 1999, B1.3.
31. Quoted in Matt Wolf, "A Director Whose Goal Is to Vanish," *New York Times,* March 28, 1999, AR9.
32. Nicholas Grene, *The Politics of Irish Drama: Plays in Context from Boucicault to Friel* (Cambridge, UK: Cambridge UP, 1999), 261.
33. Matthew Johnson, *An Archaeology of Capitalism* (Oxford UK: Blackwell, 1996), 2.
34. Ibid., 72.
35. Duffy, *Exploring the History and Heritage of Irish Landscapes*, 13.
36. John Brinckerhoff Jackson, *Discovering the Vernacular Landscape* (New Haven: Yale UP, 1984), x.
37. Conor McPherson, quoted in Victoria White, "Telling Stories in the Dark," in *Irish Times* (July 2, 1998). See also "Conor McPherson on *The Seafarer*," Abbey Theatre website, www.abbeytheatre.ie/literary/article/conor_mcpherson_on_the_seafarer (assessed March 8, 2010).
38. Ibid.
39. Nicholas Thomas, *Colonialism's Culture: Anthropology, Travel, and Government* (Princeton: Princeton UP, 1994), 6.
40. McPherson, "Late Nights," 45.
41. "An Interview with Conor McPherson," http://www.thelowry.com/shows/seafarer.html (accessed 8 April 2007).
42. Margaret Llewellyn-Jones suggests that Brendan, as the youngest, "Does not yet need to tell stories." *Contemporary Irish Drama and Cultural Identity* (Bristol UK: Intellect Books, 2002), 98.
43. Conor McPherson, "An Interview with Conor McPherson," in Gerald C. Wood, *Conor McPherson: Imagining Mischief* (Dublin: Liffey Press, 2003), 143.
44. Quoted in Mervyn Rothstein, "The Subject Is Fear and the Excess It Breeds," review of *Dublin Carol, New York Times,* February 16, 2003, AR7.
45. For extensive analysis of similar themes, see Una Chaudhuri, *Staging Place: The Geography of Modern Drama* (Ann Arbor: Michigan UP, 1997). Chaudhuri

focuses primarily on English and American texts and coins the term *geopathology* to refer to the "problem of place—and place *as problem,*" which she argues "informs realist drama deeply" (p. 55, emphasis in original).
46. Gerry Smyth, *Space and the Irish Cultural Imagination* (New York: Palgrave, 2001), 24–92.
47. Carol Christ, *Diving Deep and Surfacing: Women Writers on Spiritual Quest* (Boston: Beacon Press, 1995).
48. Henry met Synge in Paris. Synge moved from Dublin to the Aran Islands; Henry moved from Belfast to Achill Island in County Mayo. The emphasis of these urbanites on the rural West is parallel to the romantic rural ideal celebrated by Éamon de Valera and incorporated in the 1937 Irish constitution.
49. McPherson, "An Interview with Conor McPherson," in Wood, 140.
50. "Pastoral Exhibits: Narrating Authenticities in Conor McPherson's *The Weir,*" in *Irish University Review* 34, no.4 (Autumn 2004): 351–68.
51. Quoted in Deane, "Production of Cultural Space in Irish Writing," 124.
52. The persistence of supernatural beings and the desire of doctors to dismiss them (or medicate those who are aware of them) are also evident in Anne Devlin's *After Easter* (1989).
53. Quoted in Anthony Roche, *Contemporary Irish Drama: From Beckett to McGuinness* (Dublin: Gill and Macmillan, 1994), 152.
54. J. Nicholas Entrikin, *The Betweenness of Place: Towards a Geography of Modernity* (Baltimore: Johns Hopkins UP, 1991), 1, 16, 43, and passim.
55. Michael Billington, extracts from a 1997 review of the Royal Court Theatre production of *The Weir*. Originally published in *The Guardian,* http://www.albemarle-london.com/weir.html (accessed July 8, 2005).

Chapter 3

1. Henri Lefebvre, *The Production of Space,* trans. Donald Nicholson-Smith (Oxford UK: Blackwell, 1991), 11.
2. See Enrica Cerquoni, "'One bog, many bogs': Theatrical Space, Visual Image and Meaning in Some Productions of Marina Carr's *By the Bog of Cats . . . ,*" for a description (and some color photographs) of particular productions, in *The Theatre of Marina Carr: "before rules was made,"* eds. Cathy Leeney and Anna McMullan (Dublin: Carysfort, 2003), 172–99.
3. Marina Carr, *By the Bog of Cats . . . ,* in *Marina Carr: Plays One* (London: Faber, 1999), 265. Further references are to this edition and are cited in parentheses. Neither the 1998 Gallery Press edition nor the program for the premiere uses the ellipsis marks that are now a standard feature of the title.
4. *Portia Coughlan* in *Marina Carr: Plays One* (London: Faber, 1999), 223. This scene, like the Ghost Fancier's early appearance in *By the Bog of Cats . . . ,* or the narrative role of Millie in *The Mai* (1994), serves to inform audiences early

on of the ultimate fates of the women on whom the dramas center. Audiences are in a position similar to that of audiences for the Greek tragedies that influenced Carr: they know the outcome well before the stage drama concludes.

5. Eli Rozik, *Generating Theatre Meaning: A Theory and Methodology of Performance Analysis* (Brighton, UK: Sussex Academic Press, 2008), 67–68. Rozik is not discussing *By the Bog of Cats*. . . .

6. Program Note for *On Raftery's Hill*. 2000 Kennedy Center Production as part of "Arts from Ireland," an Irish Arts Festival.

7. "Interview with Mike Murphy," http2.arts.gla.ac.uk/SESLL/EngLit/ugrad/hons/IrishLit/Carr/interview.rtf (accessed June 2006). Reprinted in *Reading the Future: Twelve Writers from Ireland in Conversation with Mike Murphy*, ed. Cliodhna Ni Anluain (Dublin: Lilliput, 2000). See also Carr's "Afterword" to *Portia Coughlan* in *The Dazzling Dark: New Irish Plays*, ed. Frank McGuinness (London: Faber, 1996), 310–11; and Eileen Battersby, "Marina of the Midlands," *Irish Times*, May 4, 2000, 15.

8. *Portia Coughlan*, 191. Much has been made of Carr's use of the Midlands dialect, which is challenging for both performers and audiences. Carr describes the dialect as having a "rough exoticism" (Afterword to *Portia Coughlan*, 310). She notes that "I spoke like that as a child" but acknowledges that the dialect is "probably not even spoken [where I grew up] much any more" ("Interview with Mike Murphy"). Olwen Fouéré, who played Hester, describes the dialect as "essential," compares it to J. M. Synge's language, and notes that both Synge and Carr claim to have used "reported speech" ("Journeys in Performance: On Playing in *The Mai* and *By the Bog of Cats* . . ." Interview with Olwen Fouéré in *The Theatre of Marina Carr*, 161). In words echoing Synge's well-known contention (in the Preface to *The Playboy of the Western World*) that he "used one or two words only" that he had not heard in the country or in his own nursery, Carr has maintained that "the best lines I've ever written are things I've heard and I've just written them down" ("Interview with Mike Murphy"). Describing the Midlands dialect in Carr's *Portia Coughlan* (1996), Cathy Leeney persuasively argues that "the distance between the dialogue and ordinary standard speech licenses an intensity of image and a colourful syntax which would, elsewhere, seem overpoetic or overwritten" ("Ireland's 'exiled' women playwrights: Teresa Deevy and Marina Carr" in *The Cambridge Companion to Twentieth-Century Irish Drama*, ed. Shaun Richards [Cambridge, UK: Cambridge UP, 2004], 159). Frank McGuinness has described Carr's language as a "physical attack on the conventions of syntax, spelling and sounds of standard English" ("Masks," Introduction to *The Dazzling Dark*, ix). Patricia Lynch notes that Carr's use of dialect "may well be one of her great contributions to Irish literature" ("Hiberno-English in the Plays of Marina Carr," *Études Irlandaises* [Autumn 2006]:110). "Reported speech" or not, this Midlands dialect seems every bit as artificial and created as Synge's language, which Gerald Fay (Frank Fay's son) described as "a unique dialect" that "has never

been spoken properly anywhere but at the Abbey" (*The Abbey Theatre: Cradle of Genius* [New York: Macmillan, 1958], 97). Nicholas Grene termed Synge's language one of "created authenticity" (*Synge: A Critical Study of the Plays* [Totowa, NJ: Rowman and Littlefield, 1975], 29). The very artificiality of Carr's dialect is part of its power, and it suits her nonmimetic world perfectly.

9. Often, Irish Acts and policies (like the 1989 Prohibition of Incitement to Hatred Act, the 1998 and 2004 Employment Equality Acts, and Equal Status Acts 2000–2004) simply sidestep the issue by including membership in the Travelling community as a separate and protected category, rather than assuming Travellers would be covered by mention of race or ethnic origins. The 2006 Equality Authority Report on "Traveller Ethnicity" argues for Traveller ethnic status, in part because international and European Union agreements will not name specific groups (as Irish legislation has done), so that without ethnic status Travellers will remain unprotected under international agreements. A 2001 Report submitted to the Council of Europe (as part of the Framework Convention for the Protection of National Minorities) stated that "while Travellers are not a Gypsy or Roma people, their long shared history, cultural values, language (Gammon, Shelta, Cant), customs and traditions make them a self-defined group, and one which is recognizable and distinct."

10. Quoted in Battersby, "Marina of the Midlands," 15.

11. The Commission on Itinerancy (1960–63), headed by then Parliamentary Secretary to the Minister for Justice, Charles Haughey, described the "plight of itinerants and their isolation by the settled community, which is becoming progressively worse" as a "serious problem" that could be solved by "absorption into the general community." Haughey himself argued in 1963 that "there can be no final solution to the problems created by itinerants until they are absorbed into the general community." Haughey's language accurately reflects the common belief in the 1960s that problems were created *by* itinerants and would cease only when itinerants ceased to be itinerants. See "Traveller Ethnicity: An Equality Authority Report" (2006), 12–13. "Myth Busters: Deconstructing Myths about the Travelling Community" is an interesting example of the challenges presented in discussions of Travellers. A 2005 DivX film produced by members of the Blanchardstown Traveller Development Group, in conjunction with "Know Racism," the Irish Anti-Racism Awareness Programme, this film challenges such perceptions as "Travellers are dirty" and "Travellers are not interested in education." By arguing that Travellers are much like settled people, the film manages to sharply narrow the distinctive marks of Traveller culture. Travellers, in fact, seem much like settled people, except that they have better jewelry. Alternatively, an interview conducted by Vincent Browne with a member of the Traveller community (*Irish Times*, January 27, 2001) reveals Browne's sense (desire?) that Travellers represent a unified community in which actions by some (in this case, the leaving of trash at Sugar Loaf Mountain, County Wicklow) are the responsibility of all. Thomas MacGréil's

1988–89 national survey (*Prejudice Revisited*) revealed that 10 percent of the adult population would deny Irish citizenship to Travellers (cited in Aoife Bhreatnach, "Travellers and the Print Media: Words and Irish Identity," *Irish Studies Review* 6, no. 3 [December,1998]: 289). If such feelings persist, they suggest that many Irish believe there is an unbridgeable gap between Travellers and the settled community. Discussing the "upsurge of agitation against travellers" in 1995, Fintan O'Toole noted the ironies involved when the Irish, "one of the most unsettled peoples in Europe," display lack of tolerance toward unsettled Travellers. O'Toole cited a survey revealing that 70 percent of Irish residents "would be reluctant to buy a house next to an itinerant" and linked the hostility to issues of class, space, and cultural change. "Hostility to Travellers Challenges Migratory Irish," *Irish Times*, June 6, 1995, 16.

12. The English-Irish child at the end of Frank McGuinness's *Mutabilitie* provides an intriguing comparison.
13. Rozik, *Generating Theatre Meaning*, 113–14. See Nicholas Grene, *The Politics of Irish Drama* (London: Cambridge UP, 1999), 264, and Patrick Lonergan, *Theatre and Globalization: Irish Drama in the Celtic Tiger Era* (New York: Palgrave Macmillan, 2010), 91, for discussion of similar issues in Irish literature.
14. Reports of the position of Traveller women vary and conflict. Synge recalled being told that in Wicklow tinkers had "great witchery" and "great knowledge of the fairies," but that they would swap women "with as much talk as if you'd be selling a cow." *Wicklow, West Kerry and Connemara* (1910) (Totowa, NY: Rowman and Littlefield, 1980), 31. In "The Wandering Tribe" Lady Gregory reported being informed that "as to marriage, some used to say they lepped the budget [a toolbag or other symbolic object], but it's more likely they have no marriage at all." Another neighbor told her that "they sell their wives to one another; I've seen that myself." Still another reported that tinkers had "no marriage" but that the women were "true to their men." *Poets and Dreamers: Studies and Translations from the Irish* (Oxford, UK: Oxford UP, 1974), 94–95. Tom Murphy, who grew up in Tuam, where 7.7 percent of the population (the highest percentage in Ireland, according to Mary Burke) is Traveller, recalled that the "mythology" of Travelling People during the 1950s was that "they never used bad language, they were strictly monogamous. . . ." Travellers were, nonetheless, scorned: "better than four-letter words of insult to one another was 'Pauper,' or 'Tinker,'" He recalls seeing "Tinkers seemingly mindlessly and, yes, drunkenly, beating up one another" or their wives and "then strutting, marching about, arms and legs splaying in displaced exhibition, eyes bulging in defiance. Defiance of what? Our morality, is it?" Travelling People embody for Murphy "The contradictions and the complexities—the extremes—in people who are ordinary and who are abject." "The Creative Process," in *Irish Writers and Their Creative Process*, eds. Jacqueline Genet and Wynne Hellegouarc'h (Gerrards Cross: Colin Smythe, 1996), 82, 85. In his study *Irish Travellers: Representations*

and Realities, Michael Hayes reports that the association of Travellers with "sexual licentiousness" coexists with "folklore that Traveller women are purer than other Irish women" (Dublin: Liffey Press, 2006), 213. Jane Helleiner's ethnographic study *Irish Travellers: Racism and the Politics of Culture* (Toronto UP, 2000) is definite about the reality of chastity among Traveller women. See esp. Chapter 6, "Gender, Racism, and the Politics of Culture." Mary Burke's *"Tinkers": Synge and the Cultural History of the Irish Traveller* (Oxford, UK: Oxford UP, 2009) provides a similarly complex discussion.

15. John Wilson Foster, "Encountering Traditions," in *Nature in Ireland: A Scientific and Cultural History*, ed. John Wilson Foster (Dublin: Lilliput, 1997), 27–28. Seamus Deane's discussion of colonizers' use of husbandry metaphors to argue the need for English cultivation to tame Irish wildness is also interesting in this context. See "Civilians and Barbarians," in *Ireland's Field Day* (London: Hutchinson, 1985), 31–42.

16. In "Mossbawn" (1974) Heaney describes his encounters with the bog near his childhood home. *Preoccupations: Selected Prose 1968–1978* (London: Faber, 1980), 17–27. His well-known poem "Bogland" (1969), like *Preoccupations*, is dedicated to the Irish artist T. P. Flanagan, for whom the bogs have also been key emblems of Ireland. In "Landscape or Mindscape? Seamus Heaney's Bogs," Dianne Meredith explores what a "humanistic approach to the study of geography" and "literary geography" add to understanding of Heaney's bog poems. *Irish Geography* 32, no. 2 (1999): 126–34.

17. Burke, *"Tinkers,"* 238, citing a 1934 *Irish Press* article, points out that the barrel-top wagons "were actually introduced to Travellers by British Romanies in the inter-war period."

18. Frank McGuinness, *The Bird Sanctuary* in *Frank McGuinness: Plays 2* (London: Faber, 2002), 342.

19. Hester's memories of her mother and brother are comparable to Medea's conclusion (in Brendan Kennelly's 1991 adaptation of Euripides's play) that "there's nothing/left but memory. Some griefs deepen/with memory, become more real/than when they happened first." Eamonn Jordan has a useful summary of other parallels between Euripides's Medea and Carr's Hester in *Dissident Dramaturgies: Contemporary Irish Theatre* (Dublin: Irish Academic Press, 2010), 161–63. See *Amid Our Troubles: Irish Versions of Greek Tragedy*, eds. Marianne McDonald and J. Michael Walton (London: Methuen, 2002) for a discussion of other Irish plays with Greek roots.

20. "Hit or Myth: The Greeks and Irish Drama," in *Amid Our Troubles*, 33.

21. M. K. Martinovich, "The Mythical and the Macabre: The Study of Greeks and Ghosts in the Shaping of the American Premiere of *By the Bog of Cats . . .*," in *Theatre of Marina Carr*, 118.

22. "'One bog, many bogs': Theatrical Space, Visual Image and Meaning in Some Productions of Marina Carr's *By the Bog of Cats . . .*," in *Theatre of Marina*

Carr, 180. Cerquoni goes on to provide specific and perceptive analyses of a number of productions of the play.
23. Hanna Scolnicov, *Woman's Theatrical Space* (Cambridge, UK: Cambridge UP, 1994).
24. See Janet Wolff, "The Invisible Flâneuse: Women and the Literature of Modernity," in ed. Andrew Benjamin, *The Problems of Modernity: Adorno and Benjamin* (London: Routledge, 1989), 141–55. Wolff demonstrates the extent to which a man is traditionally free to stroll urban areas, seeking experience and understanding, whereas a woman is not. The masculine form *flâneur* thus becomes the norm, and the feminine form *flâneuse* is a rare exception.
25. Shirley Ardener, "Ground Rules and Social Maps for Women: An Introduction," in *Women and Space: Ground Rules and Social Maps*, ed. Shirley Ardenar (Oxford, UK: Berg Publications, 1992), 1–2.
26. Susan Griffin, Preface to 1999 edition of *Woman and Nature: The Roaring Inside Her* (1978) (San Francisco: Sierra Club Books, 1999), ix.
27. See Gillian Rose, *Feminism and Geography: The Limits of Geographical Knowledge* (Minneapolis: U of Minnesota P, 1993), 105–106 and passim.
28. The 1937 Irish Constitution regularly described women's role as "in the home" and incorporated many attitudes common in the Catholic church, to which most residents belonged. A number of essays in *Women in Irish Drama: A Century of Authorship and Representation*, ed. Melissa Sihra (Basingstoke, UK: Palgrave, 2007) reflect on the confinement of women to interior space. See, in particular, Cathy Leeney's "The Space Outside: Images of Women in Plays by Eva Gore-Booth and Dorothy Macardle" and Enrica Cerquoni's "Women in Rooms: Landscapes of the Missing in Anne Devlin's *Ourselves Alone*." The Introduction of this fine collection is by Marina Carr.
29. The connection with Hawthorne's Hester is strengthened by Olwen Fouéré's revelation that in early drafts of Carr's play Hester Swane's name was Angel. "Journeys in Performance," 162. Townspeople in Hawthorne's novel ended by interpreting the A on Hester Prynne's breast as "Angel."
30. As Hawthorne well knew, Puritans were not the black-and-white clad Pilgrims familiar from stereotypical US Thanksgiving images, yet in his novel the scarlet letter (which gleams on Hester's breast and in the night sky and on the tombstone) is a visual punctuation in the novel's world, which is dominated by the color black (except for the remarkable use of green in relation to Pearl).
31. I am grateful to Leslie Durham for expanding my thinking here.
32. Matthew Johnson, *An Archaeology of Capitalism* (Oxford, UK: Blackwell, 1996), 84.
33. In "Virgin Mother Ireland" Gerardine Meaney explores the extent to which the "conflated" images of Mother Ireland and the Virgin Mary provided a "fusion of national and religious iconography" into an image of a white, still,

and "singularly unmaternal" figure, in *Gender, Ireland, and Cultural Change: Race, Sex, and Nation* (New York: Routledge, 2010), 3–20.
34. For a full discussion, see Elizabeth Butler Cullingford, "British Romans and Irish Carthaginians: Anticolonial Metaphor in Heaney, Friel, and McGuinness," *PMLA* 111, no. 2 (March 1996): 222–39.
35. Programme Note (Abbey Theatre 1998). Reprinted in *Theatre of Marina Carr*, 88.
36. Burke, *"Tinkers,"* 106.
37. "Journeys in Performance," 164.
38. *Low in the Dark*, in *Marina Carr: Plays 1*, 5.
39. "Journeys in Performance," 171.
40. Lonergan, *Theatre and Globalization*, 173.
41. Roland Barthes, *The Fashion System* (1967), trans. Matthew Ward and Richard Howard (New York: Hill and Wang, 1983), 15.
42. Keir Elam has summarized the impact of such theatrical "signs" as costume, which audiences "inevitably" relate "to the social, moral, and ideological values operative in the community of which performers and spectators are part." *The Semiotics of Theatre and Drama* (New York: Methuen, 1980), 10.
43. Martinovich, "Mythical and the Macabre," 119.
44. "On the Study of Celtic Literature," in *Lectures and Essays in Criticism*, ed. R. H. Super (Ann Arbor: U of Michigan P, 1962), 347.
45. Maria-Elena Doyle, "A Spindle for the Battle: Feminism, Myth, and the Woman-Nation in Irish Revival Drama," *Theatre Journal* 51, no. 1 (1999): 34.
46. *Waiting for Godot*: "A country road. A tree. Evening." *Happy Days*: "Expanse of scorched grass rising centre to low mound. . . . Maximum of simplicity and symmetry." *Act Without Words I*: "Desert. Dazzling light." *Rough for Theatre I*: "Street corner. Ruins." *By the Bog of Cats . . . :* "Dawn. On the Bog of Cats. A bleak white landscape of ice and snow."
47. Henri Lefebvre, *The Production of Space* (1974), trans. Donald Nicholson-Smith (Oxford, UK: Blackwell, 1991), 26–31 and passim.
48. Quoted in Battersby, "Marina of the Midlands." Emphasis added.
49. *The "Tinkers" in Irish Literature: Unsettled subjects and the construction of difference* (Dublin: Irish Academic Press, 2008), 64–65.
50. Burke, *"Tinkers,"* 14, 190.
51. See, for example, Vic Merriman, "Decolonization Postponed: The Theatre of Tiger Trash," *Irish University Review* 24, no. 2 (Autumn/Winter 1999): 305–17.
52. Figures in "Misli, Crush, Misli: Irish Travellers and Nomadism," by Mark Donahue, Robbie McVeigh, and Maureen Ward, suggest that in both the Republic and Northern Ireland, the percentage of Travellers who self-report being "on the road" hovers between 20 and 25 percent. The authors acknowledge the difficulty of surveying Travellers, and thus the uncertainty of such

statistics (which were collected in 2001 and 2002). But they believe these figures are generally accurate. "Misli, Crush, Misli," from Gammon (Shelta, or Cant), the Irish Traveller language, is translated "Go, Move, Shift." http://www.itmtrav.com/publications/MisliCrushMisli.html (accessed March 28, 2007). Hayes, *Irish Travellers,* 89, and Sinéad ní Shúinéar, "History as Dialogue: An Anthropological Perspective," in *Portraying Irish Travellers: Histories and Representations,* ed. Ciara Breathnach and Aoife Bhreatnach (Cambridge, UK: Cambridge Scholars Press, 2006), 71, agree that estimates of the total number of Irish Travellers varies, but put the number at approx. 24,000–28,000 in the Republic (approximately 0.5percent of the population). Hayes reports an estimate of 1,500 Travellers in Northern Ireland.

53. As a 1987 European Commission report on "School Provision for Gypsy and Traveller Children" (Luxembourg, 1987) put it, "Nomadism is as much a state of mind as a state of fact" (34–35). Or, as Traveller Michael McDonagh explained, "Travellers who are not moving can, and do, retain the mindset of a nomad." "Nomadism in Irish Travellers' Identity," in *Irish Travellers: Culture and Ethnicity,* eds. May McCann, Séamus Ó Síocháin and Joseph Ruane (Belfast: Institute of Irish Studies, 1994), 98. Helleiner's ethnographic study supports this conclusion. See esp. Chapter 4, "Travelling, Racism, and the Politics of Culture."

54. The 2007 U.S. television series *The Riches* uses, in connection with U.S. Travellers, familiar stereotypes that are missing in Hester's life. The Riches are grifters who make their living by craft and con; they move regularly (often one step ahead of the law); they belong to a community they refer to as "the family"; they distrust formal education; they are casual about their impact on the environment; they own no real estate. The Traveller community to which they belong has a tendency toward violence and marries its young women off at an early age. Like Hester, though, the Riches yearn (albeit not without mixed feelings) for a more settled life, which they seek to acquire by fraud. Similar stereotypes drive films like *Traveller* (1997, starring Bill Paxton and set in the US South) and *Trojan Edie* (1997, starring Stephen Rea and Richard Harris and set in Ireland).

55. It is also, of course, an example of a common trope in Irish myth and literature, which frequently depict humans (usually women) changed into swans. Carr discussed both mythological swans and the swans she encountered growing up by a Midlands lake in her 2000 interview with Mike Murphy. Her account of an exchange with swans (whom she links to the death of her mother) after a lapse of years may be the seed for the play's tale of Hester's recognition by a swan after a lapse of years.

56. The distinction is made by John Brinckerhoff Jackson, *Discovering the Vernacular Landscape* (New Haven: Yale UP, 1984).

57. Quoted in J. Nicholas Entrikin, *The Betweenness of Place: Towards a Geography of Modernity* (Baltimore: Johns Hopkins UP, 1991), xi.
58. Frank Mitchell and Michael Ryan, *Reading the Irish Landscape* (Dublin: Town House, 1993), 346.
59. Carr, the second oldest of six children, lost her mother when she was 17.
60. "Staging Histories in Marina Carr's Midlands Plays," *Irish University Review* 36, no.2 (September 2006): 389–403.
61. "Landscape and the Celtic Soul," *Éire-Ireland* 31, no.3 (Fall/Winter 1997): 228–54.
62. Lonergan, in *Theatre and Globalization,* provides a full analysis of these and multiple other aspects of globalization.
63. Michael Hayes cites estimates that approximately 28,000 residents of the Irish Republic self-identify as Travellers, and that another 1,500 live in Northern Ireland. "Indigenous Otherness: Some Aspects of Irish Traveller Social History," *Éire-Ireland* 41, nos. 3 and 4 (Fall/Winter 2006): 135.
64. Frank O'Connor, *The Lonely Voice: A Study of the Short Story* (Cleveland: World Publishing, 1963), 156.
65. Marina Carr, *By the Bog of Cats* (Loughcrew, Ireland: Gallery Press, 1998), 77.
66. In *Specters of Marx: The State of the Debt, the Work of Mourning, and the New International* (New York: Routledge, 1994), Jacques Derrida notes that the past is a necessary definer of the present and that the future depends on coming to terms with the Other. Punning on *ontology,* he coins *hauntology* as the term for these necessary conjunctions. Carr's play benefits from consideration in light of Derrida's theory.
67. Hayes, *Irish Travellers,* 259.
68. Afterword to *Portia Coughlan,* 310–11.
69. "Reflections Across Water: New Stages of Performing Carr," in *Theatre of Marina Carr,* 100.

Chapter 4

1. Frank McGuinness, *Gates of Gold* (London: Faber, 2002). All references are to this text and are cited in parentheses. I have also discussed this play's use of space in *Contexts for Frank McGuinness's Drama* (Washington, DC: Catholic UP, 2004) and in "Spatial Metaphors in Frank McGuinness's *Gates of Gold,*" *Études Irlandaises* 29, no. 2 (Autumn 2004): 151–64.
2. Maurice Fitzpatrick, "Interview with Frank McGuinness," March 18, 2009, http://www.mauicefitzpatrick.org (accessed December 18, 2010).
3. John O'Mahony, "A Happy Marriage," Interview with Frank McGuinness, *The Guardian* (April 24, 2008), http://www.guardian.co.uk/stage/2008/apr/24/theatre1 (accessed May 2, 2009).

4. Una Chaudhuri, *Staging Place: The Geography of Modern Drama* (Ann Arbor: Michigan UP, 1997), 27.
5. Numerous recent studies, many building on work by Freud and Kate Millet, explore the relationship of space and sexuality. See Nancy Duncan, ed. *BodySpace: Destabilizing Geographies of Gender and Sexuality* (London: Routledge, 1996); Gillian Rose, *Feminism and Geography: The Limits of Geographical Knowledge* (Minneapolis: U Minnesota P, 1993); Elizabeth Wilson, *The Sphinx in the City: Urban Life, the Control of Disorder, and Women* (Berkeley: U California P, 1991); Beatriz Colomina, ed., *Sexuality and Space* (Princeton, NJ: Princeton Architectural Press, 1992); ed. Scott Brewster, et al., *Ireland in Proximity: History, Gender, Space* (London: Routledge, 1999); and Wendy Wall, *Staging Domesticity: Household Work and English Identity in Early Modern Drama* (Cambridge, UK: Cambridge UP, 2002).
6. Henri Lefebvre, *The Production of Space*, trans. Donald Nicholson-Smith (Oxford, UK: Blackwell, 1991), 14.
7. Christopher Fitz-Simon's *The Boys: A Biography of Micheál MacLíammóir and Hilton Edwards* (Dublin: New Island Books, 2002) is a comprehensive guide. In the 1930s the Gate nurtured young actors like James Mason, Orson Welles, and Cyril Cusack. In the 1950s, Siobhán McKenna was associated with it. McGuinness incorporates details from the lives of the founders: the wearing of a wig; offstage use of makeup; the discarding of both wig and makeup in the face of age and illness; connections with Africa and Spain; references to Maupassant. Directly paralleling an episode recalled in Fitz-Simon's biography (267), McGuinness has Conrad respond to phone requests for "Dr. Gabriel" (after Gabriel had received an honorary degree) with an offer of "Nurse Conrad" instead (49). McGuinness has recalled the power of MacLíammóir's one-man show *The Importance of Being Oscar*, which was one of his earliest theater experiences. And he has noted the impact on him of Edwards's funeral oration for MacLíammóir (a recitation of the funeral dirge from *Cymbeline* IV, ii, 258–81).
8. Hilton Edwards directed the premiere of *Philadelphia, Here I Come!*
9. "The House Image in Three Contemporary Irish Plays," *New Hibernia Review* 8 (Summer 2004): 64–84.
10. "Declan Hughes in Conversation with Ryan Tubridy," *Theatre Talk: Voices of Irish Theatre Practitioners*, ed. Lilian Chambers et al. (Dublin: Carysfort Press, 2001), 181.
11. Anthony Roche, *Contemporary Irish Drama: From Beckett to McGuinness* (Dublin: Gill and Macmillan, 1994), 270.
12. Fitz-Simon, *The Boys*, 288.
13. In "The Healing Touch," an interview with Joe Jackson, *The Irish Sunday Independent* 21 (April 2002), http:///www.alanhoward.org.uk/mcguinness.htm (accessed November 2010).

14. Quoted in Gaston Bachelard, *The Poetics of Space* (1958), trans. Maria Jolas (Boston: Beacon Press, 1994), 29.
15. I am grateful to Philip Tilling for identifying the source of the portrait.
16. Fitz-Simon, *Boys,* 218.
17. John Brinckerhoff Jackson, *Discovering the Vernacular Landscape* (New Haven: Yale UP, 1984), 3.
18. See Simon Schama, *Landscape and Memory* (New York: Knopf, 1995) for a full discussion of Magritte's painting.
19. The set for the London premiere (at Finborough Theatre in December 2004) "evok[ed] an old-fashioned theatre foyer—full of gold detail and gilt-framed pictures," and the bedroom mirror had lights like a dressing table (reviews @fringereport.com, December 3, 2004). Those set details would have altered the impact of the lighting. Photographs indicate that the set for this production (which transferred to other theaters) was generally more elaborate than the one used in the Gate production.
20. McGuinness's *Innocence: The Life and Death of Michelangelo Merisi, Caravaggio* (1986) has two parts: "Life" and "Death."
21. *Quad* in Samuel Beckett, *The Complete Dramatic Works* (London: Faber, 1986), 449–54.
22. Lefebvre, *Production of Space,* 41, 59.
23. Michel Foucault, *The History of Sexuality: An Introduction,* trans. Robert Hurley (New York: Vintage Books, 1990), 1:4.
24. *Irish Theatre Forum* 3, no.1 (Spring 1999), http://www.ucd.ie/irthfrm/issue52.htm (accessed January 27, 2009). Smyth's analysis was done before *Gates of Gold* appeared, but his discussion of texts like Tom Murphy's *Bailegangaire* and Samuel Beckett's *Eh Joe* (1965) and *Footfalls* (1975) sheds light on *Gates.* And though Smyth does not mention them, both McGuinness's *The Factory Girls* and Friel's *Wonderful Tennessee* involve parallel constructions of bed spaces.
25. Imelda Foley, *The Girls in the Big Picture: Gender in Contemporary Ulster Theatre* (Belfast: Blackstaff, 2003), 111 and 115.
26. Ibid.,125. *Gates of Gold* was not part of Foley's consideration.
27. "Camping in Utopia: Frank McGuinness's *Carthaginians* and the queer aesthetic," *New Voices in Irish Criticism* 5, eds. Ruth Connolly and Ann Coughlan. (Dublin: Four Courts, 2005), 24–41.
28. Michel Foucault, "Of Other Spaces, Heterotopias" (1967, 1984), trans. Jay Miskowiec, http://foucault.info/documents/heteroTopia/foucault.heteroTopia.en.html (accessed February 8, 2011).
29. Ibid.
30. "The Spaces of Irish Drama," in *Kaleidoscopic Views of Ireland,* eds. Munira H. Mutran and Laura P. Z. Izasrra (São Paulo: U de São Paulo P, 2003), 64, 59. Grene's discussion of Brian Friel's *Philadelphia, Here I Come!* and *Faith Healer* have interesting connections with the issues I am discussing here.

31. "'Isn't it just like real life?': Frank McGuinness and the (Re)writing of Stage Space," *Canadian Journal of Irish Studies* 20, no.1 (July 1994): 61–62.
32. Brian Singleton. "Notes from a New Country," *Irish Theatre Magazine* 30 (2007): 59.
33. Alma also hums "I Dreamt I Dwelt in Marble Halls," a song James Joyce used in *Finnigan's Wake* and in two of the *Dubliners* stories ("Eveline" and "Clay").
34. "Frank McGuinness in Conversation with Joseph Long," in *Theatre Talk: Voices of Irish Theatre Practitioners*, eds. Lilian Chambers, Ger FitzGibbon, and Eamonn Jordan (Dublin: Carysfort, 2001), 103.
35. "Interview with Frank McGuinness" in Foley, *Girls in the Big Picture*, 108.
36. McGuinness, Lecture at Trinity College Dublin (1991), quoted in Foley, *Girls in the Big Picture*, 106. McGuinness was talking about his 1988 play *Carthaginians*.
37. "After Ireland: The Death of a National Literature?," Irish Seminar Keynote Lecture, National Gallery of Ireland (Dublin), June 25, 2009. Nicholas de Jongh made similar comments about the de-Irishification of McGuinness's work in a *London Evening Standard* review of *There Came a Gypsy Riding*, which he noted "could easily be mistaken for an old-fashioned country house drama in Shaftesbury Avenue starring Ralph Richardson," http://www.theatre.com (accessed August 7, 2007).
38. Bachelard, *Poetics of Space*, 5.
39. Ibid., 132.
40. Brian Singleton's analysis of other McGuinness plays helps to open up *Gates of Gold*. See "Queer Eye for the Irish Guy: Transgressive Sexualities and the Performance of Nation," in *The Dreaming Body: Contemporary Irish Theatre*, eds. Melissa Sihra and Paul Murphy (Gerrards Cross, UK: Colin Smythe, 2009), 99–113.
41. See David Krasner, "Empathy and Theater," in *Staging Philosophy: Intersections of Theater, Performance, and Philosophy*, eds. David Krasner and David Z. Saltz (Ann Arbor: Michigan UP, 2006), 256. Emphasis in original.
42. Gillian Rose, *Feminism and Geography: The Limits of Geographical Knowledge* (Minneapolis: U of Minnesota P, 1993), 47.
43. Foucault dates "repeated attempts, by various means, to reduce all of sex to its reproductive function, its heterosexual and adult form, and its matrimonial legitimacy" to the Victorian era, when "Sexuality . . . moved into the home . . . A single locus of sexuality was acknowledged in social space as well as at the heart of every household, but it was a utilitarian and fertile one: the parents' bedroom." *History of Sexuality*, 103, 3.
44. How obvious the wig should be, before Gabriel discards it, is an intriguing production issue. The English premiere (London's Finborough Theatre, 2004) opened with Gabriel (William Gaunt) applying black dye to the white hair

escaping from under his wig, which eliminated the possibility that audiences would be surprised by Gabriel's later discarding of the wig.
45. Joseph Allen Boone, *Libidinal Currents: Sexuality and the Shaping of Modernism* (Chicago: U of Chicago P, 1998), 151–72.
46. Rose, *Feminism and Geography*, 146.
47. Seamus Heaney, "The Sense of Place," in *Preoccupations* (London: Faber, 1980), 132.
48. Martin Heidegger, "Building Dwelling Thinking," in *Poetry, Language, Thought*, trans. Albert Hofstadter (New York: Harper Colophon, 1971). Emphasis in original.
49. David Norris, represented by Mary Robinson (later president of Ireland), won a case before the European Court of Human Rights in 1988, but the sexual code for Irish gays and straights was not equalized until the 1993 Sexual Offenses Act, worked on by Norris, who was by then an Irish senator.
50. Lefebvre, *Production of Space*, 116.
51. Michael G. Cronin argues that "incorporation of the southern Irish lesbian and gay political movement within a conception of national progress" means that "gay identity has been emptied of any radical political potential." See "'He's My Country': Liberalism, Nationalism and Sexuality in Contemporary Irish Gay Fiction," *Éire-Ireland* 39, nos. 3 and 4 (Fall/Winter 2004): 251, 254.
52. Essays focused on various aspects of this issue are included in *Sex, Nation, and Dissent in Irish Writing*, ed. Éibhear Walshe (Cork: Cork UP, 1997).

Conclusion

1. Nicholas Grene, *The Politics of Irish Drama: Plays in Context from Boucicault to Friel* (Cambridge, UK: Cambridge UP, 1999), 262–63.
2. There are Irish weirs in addition to the one on the Shannon, but McPherson's text makes it clear which weir he has in mind. The Bog of Cats does not exist, but roughly one-sixth of the island of Ireland is bog, and legend has it that a black cat once roamed the bogs. The Gate Theatre is clearly among the references implied by *Gates of Gold*.
3. Una Chaudhuri. *Staging Place: The Geography of Modern Drama* (Ann Arbor: Michigan UP, 1995), 20.
4. Eric Bentley. *In Search of Theater* (New York: Alfred Knopf, 1953), 327.
5. Ibid., 321.
6. Ibid., 227–28.
7. Fintan O'Toole, "Shadows over Ireland," in *American Theatre* 15 (July/August 1998): 18–19.
8. Ibid. 19.
9. Anthony Roche, *Contemporary Irish Drama: From Beckett to McGuinness* (Dublin: Gill and Macmillan, 1994), 279–80.

10. Patrick Lonergan, *Theatre and Globalization: Irish Drama in the Celtic Tiger Era* (New York: Palgrave Macmillan, 2010), 148.
11. Ibid., 162.
12. Frank McGuinness, *Dolly West's Kitchen*. *Frank McGuinness: Plays 2* (London: Faber, 2002), 210.

Bibliography

Andrews, J. H. *A Paper Landscape: The Ordnance Survey in Nineteenth-Century Ireland* (1975). Dublin: Four Courts, 2002.

Ardener, Shirley, ed. *Women and Space: Ground Rules and Social Maps*. Oxford, UK: Berg Publications, 1992.

Arnold, Matthew. "On the Study of Celtic Literature." In *Lectures and Essays in Criticism*. Edited by R. H. Super. Ann Arbor: U of Michigan P, 1962.

Artaud, Antonin. *The Theater and Its Double* (1958). Translated by Mary Caroline Richards. New York: Grove/Evergreen, 1979.

Bachelard, Gaston. *The Poetics of Space* (1958). Translated by Maria Jolas. Boston: Beacon Press, 1994.

Barthes, Roland. *The Fashion System* (1967). Translated by Matthew Ward and Richard Howard. New York: Hill and Wang, 1983.

Battersby, Eileen. "Marina of the Midlands," *Irish Times*, May 4, 2000, 15.

Beckett, Samuel. *The Complete Dramatic Works*. London: Faber, 1986.

Bentley, Eric. *In Search of Theater*. New York: Alfred Knopf, 1953.

Bhreatnach, Aoife. "Travellers and the Pring Media: Words and Irish Identity." *Irish Studies Review* 6, no.3 (December 1998), 285–90.

Bhreatnach, Aoife and Ciara Bhreatnach, eds. *Portraying Irish Travellers: Histories and Representations*. Cambridge: Cambridge Scholars, 2006.

Billington, Michael. Review of *The Weir*. *The Guardian* (1997). http://www.albemarle-london.com/weir.html (accessed July 8, 2005).

Boone, Joseph Allen. *Libidinal Currents: Sexuality and the Shaping of Modernism*. Chicago: U of Chicago P, 1998.

Borges, Jorge Luis, *A Universal History of Infamy*. Translated by Norman Thomas di Giovanni. New York: Penguin, 1975.

Brewster, Scott, Virginia Crossman, Fiona Becket, and David Alderson, eds. *Ireland in Proximity: History, Gender, Space*. London: Routledge, 1999.

Burke, Mary. *"Tinkers": Synge and the Cultural History of the Irish Traveller*. Oxford, UK: Oxford UP, 2009.

Carleton, William. *Traits and Stories of the Irish Peasantry (1842–4)*. Project Gutenberg E-Book #16014. Accessed September 2008.

Carlson, Marvin. *Places of Performance: The Semiotics of Theatre Architecture*. Ithaca, NY: Cornell UP, 1989.

Carr, Marina. "Afterword to *Portia Coughlan*." *The Dazzling Dark: New Irish Plays*. 310–11. Edited by Frank McGuinness. London: Faber, 1996.

———. *By the Bog of Cats*. Loughcrew, Ireland: Gallery Press, 1998.

———. *By the Bog of Cats . . .* In *Plays 1*. London: Faber and Faber, 1999. 257–341.

———. *Low in the Dark* in *Marina Carr: Plays 1*. London: Faber, 1999. 1–99.

Carroll, Lewis. *The Complete Sylvie and Bruno* (1893). San Francisco: Mercury House, 1991.

Cashman, John. *Probing the Past for the Present: The Northern Irish Border: Character and Community*. Bloomington: Indiana UP, 2009.

Chambers, Lilian, Ger Fitzgibbon, and Eamonn Jordan, eds. *Theatre Talk: Voices of Irish Theatre Practitioners*. Dublin: Carysfort Press, 2001.

Chaudhuri, Una. *Staging Place: The Geography of Modern Drama*. Ann Arbor: Michigan UP, 1997.

Christ, Carol. *Diving Deep and Surfacing: Women Writers on Spiritual Quest*. Boston: Beacon Press, 1995.

Colomina, Beatriz, ed. *Sexuality and Space*. Princeton, NJ: Princeton Architectural Press, 1992.

Connolly, Ruth, and Ann Coughlan, eds. *New Voices in Irish Criticism 5*. Dublin: Four Courts Press, 2005.

Cronin, Michael G. "'He's My Country': Liberalism, Nationalism and Sexuality in Contemporary Irish Gay Fiction." *Éire-Ireland* 39, nos. 3 and 4 (Fall/Winter 2004): 250–67.

Cullen, Fintan. *Visual Politics: The Representation of Ireland 1750–1930*. Cork, Ireland: Cork UP, 1997.

Cullingford, Elizabeth. "British Romans and Irish Carthaginians: Anticolonial Metaphor in Heaney, Friel, and McGuinness." *PMLA* 111, no. 2 (March 1996): 222–39.

Deane, Seamus. "Civilians and Barbarians." In *Ireland's Field Day*. London: Hutchinson, 1985, 33–42.

———. "The Production of Cultural Space in Irish Writing." *boundary 2* 21, no. 3 (1994): 117–44.

Derrida, Jacques. *Specters of Marx: The State of the Debt, the Work of Mourning, and the New International* (1993). Translated by Peggy Kamuf. London: Routledge, 1994.

Doherty, Gillian M. *The Irish Ordnance Survey: History, Culture and Memory*. Dublin: Four Courts Press, 2004.

Donahue, Mark, Robbie McVeigh, and Maureen Ward. "Misli, Crush, Misli: Irish Travellers and Nomadism." http://www.itmtrav.com/publications/MisliCrushMisli.html (accessed March 28, 2007).

Dowling, P. J. *The Hedge Schools of Ireland* (1935). Cork: Mercier Press, 1968.

Doyle, Maria-Elena. "A Spindle for the Battle: Feminism, Myth, and the Woman-Nation in Irish Revival Drama." *Theatre Journal* 51, no. 1 (1999): 33–46.

Duffy, Patrick. *Exploring the History and Heritage of Irish Landscapes*. Dublin: Four Courts Press, 2007.

Duncan, Nancy, ed. *BodySpace: Destabilizing Geographies of Gender and Sexuality*. London: Routledge, 1996.

Elam, Keir. *The Semiotics of Theatre and Drama*. New York: Methuen, 1980.

Eliot, T. S. *On Poetry and Poets* (1951). New York: Noonday Press, 1961.

Entrikin, J. Nicholas. *The Betweenness of Place: Towards a Geography of Modernity*. Baltimore: Johns Hopkins UP, 1991.

Fáilte Ireland and the Heritage Council. *Climate Change, Heritage and Tourism: Implications for Ireland's Coast and Inland Waterways: Summary Document.* Dublin: Heritage Council of Ireland Series, 2009.

Fischer-Lichte, Erika. *The Semiotics of Theater.* Translated by Jeremy Gaines. Bloomington: Indiana UP, 1992.

Fitz-Simon, Christopher. *The Boys: A Biography of Micheál MacLiammóir and Hilton Edwards.* Dublin: New Island Books, 2002.

Flannery, James. "W. B. Yeats and the Abbey Theatre Company." *Educational Theatre Journal* 27, no. 2 (May 1975): 179–96.

Foley, Imelda. *The Girls in the Big Picture: Gender in Contemporary Ulster Theatre.* Belfast, UK: Blackstaff Press, 2003.

Foster, John Wilson, ed. *Nature in Ireland: A Scientific and Cultural History.* Dublin: Lilliput Press, 1997.

Foucault, Michel. *The History of Sexuality: An Introduction.* Translated by Robert Hurley. New York: Vintage Books, 1990.

———. "Of Other Spaces, Heterotopias." (1967 and 1984). http://foucault.info/document/heteroTopia/foucault.heteroTopia.en.html (accessed February 6, 2011).

Frawley, Oona. *Irish Pastoral: Nostalgia and Twentieth-Century Irish Literature.* Dublin: Irish Academic Press, 2005.

Friel, Brian. *Translations.* London: Faber and Faber, 1981.

Genet, Jacqueline, and Wynne Hellegouarc'h. *Irish Writers and Their Creative Process.* Gerrards Cross, UK: Colin Smythe, 1996.

Gleitman, Claire. "'Isn't It Just Like Real Life?': Frank McGuinness and the (Re)writing of Stage Space." *Canadian Journal of Irish Studies* 20, no.1 (July 1994), 60–73.

Goldstrom, J. M. *The Social Content of Education: 1808–1870: A Study of the Working Class School Reader in England and Ireland.* Shannon: Irish UP, 1972.

Graham, Brian. *In Search of Ireland: A Cultural Geography.* London: Routledge, 1997.

Gregory, Lady Augusta. *Poets and Dreamers: Studies and Translations from the Irish.* Oxford, UK: Oxford UP, 1974.

Grene, Nicholas. *The Politics of Irish Drama: Plays in Context from Boucicault to Friel.* Cambridge: Cambridge UP, 1999.

———. *Synge: A Critical Study of the Plays.* Totowa, NJ: Rowman and Littlefield, 1975.

Griffin, Susan. "Preface," *Woman and Nature: The Roaring Inside Her.* San Francisco: Sierra Club Books, 1999.

Hawkes, Terence. *Meaning by Shakespeare.* London: Routledge, 1992.

Hayes, Michael. "Indigenous Otherness: Some Aspects of Irish Traveller Social History." *Éire-Ireland* 41, nos. 3 and 4 (Fall/Winter 2006): 133–61.

———. *Irish Travellers: Representations and Realities.* Dublin: Liffey Press, 2006.

Heaney, Seamus. *Finders Keepers: Selected Prose 1971–2001.* New York: Farrar Straus, 2002.

———. *Preoccupations: Selected Prose 1968–1978.* London: Faber and Faber, 1980.

Heidigger, Martin. *Poetry, Language, Thought.* Translated by Albert Hofstadter. New York: Harper Colophon, 1971.

Helleiner, Jane. *Irish Travellers: Racism and the Politics of Culture.* Toronto: Toronto UP, 2000.

Hill, Leslie, and Helen Paris, eds. *Performance and Place.* New York: Palgrave Macmillan, 2006.

Hirsch, Edward. "The Imaginary Irish Peasant." *PMLA* 106, no. 5 (October 1991): 1116–33.

Hornby, Richard. *Script into Performance: A Structuralist Approach.* New York: Paragon House, 1987.

Hynes, Garry. "Accepting the Fiction of Being 'National.'" *Irish Times* (May 3, 1993).

Issacharoff, Michael. *Discourse as Performance.* Stanford, CA: Stanford UP, 1989.

Issacharoff, Michael, and Robin F. Jones, eds. *Performing Texts.* Philadelphia: U of Pennsylvania Press, 1988.

Jackson, John Brinckerhoff. *Discovering the Vernacular Landscape.* New Haven, CT: Yale UP, 1984.

Johnson, Matthew. *An Archaeology of Capitalism.* Oxford, UK: Blackwell, 1996.

Jordan, Eamonn. *Dissident Dramaturgies: Contemporary Irish Theatre.* Dublin: Irish Academic Press, 2010.

———. "Pastoral Exhibits: Narrating Authenticities in Conor McPherson's *The Weir.*" *Irish University Review* 34, no. 4 (Autumn 2004): 351–68.

———, ed. *Theatre Stuff: Critical Essays on Contemporary Irish Theatre.* Dublin: Carysfort Press, 2000.

Kennedy, S. B. *Paul Henry*. New Haven, CT: Yale UP, 2007.

Kiberd, Declan. *Inventing Ireland: The Literature of the Modern Nation*. London: Jonathan Cape, 1995.

———. *The Irish Writer and the World*. Cambridge: Cambridge UP, 2005.

Klein, Bernhard. *Maps and the Writing of Space in Early Modern England and Ireland*. New York: Palgrave Macmillan, 2001.

Krasner, David, and David Z. Saltz, eds. *Staging Philosophy: Intersections of Theater, Performance, and Philosophy*. Ann Arbor: Michigan UP, 2006.

Lanters, José. *The "Tinkers" in Irish Literature: Unsettled Subjects and the Construction of Difference*. Dublin: Irish Academic Press, 2008.

Leeney, Cathy, and Anna McMullan. *The Theatre of Marina Carr: "Before Rules Was Made."* Dublin: Carysfort Press, 2003.

Lefebvre, Henri. *The Production of Space*. Translated by Donald Nicholson-Smith. Oxford, UK: Blackwell, 1991.

Llewellyn-Jones, Margaret. *Contemporary Irish Drama and Cultural Identity*. Briston, UK: Intellect Books, 2002.

Lojek, Helen. "Brian Friel's Plays and George Steiner's Linguistics: Translating the Irish." *Contemporary Literature* 35 (Spring 1994): 83–99. Reprinted in *Contemporary Literary Criticism* 115: 239–45.

———. "Space in Wonderful Tennessee." *Irish Theatre International* 2, no. 1 (August 2009): 48–61.

Lonergan, Patrick. *Theatre and Globalization: Irish Drama in the Celtic Tiger Era*. New York: Palgrave Macmillan, 2010.

Lynch, Patricia. "Hiberno-English in the Plays of Marina Carr." *Études Irlandaises* 31, no. 2 (Autumn 2006): 109–23.

Mahon, Derek. *Collected Poems*. Loughcrew, Ireland: Gallery Press, 1999.

McAuley, Gay. *Space in Performance: Making Meaning in the Theatre*. Ann Arbor: Michigan UP, 1999.

McCann, May, and Séamus Ó Síocháin and Joseph Ruane, eds. *Irish Travellers: Culture and Ethnicity*. Belfast: Institute of Irish Studies, 1994.

McDonald, Marianne, and J. Michael Walton, eds. *Amid Our Troubles: Irish Versions of Greek Tragedy*. London: Methuen, 2002.

McGuinness, Frank. *The Bird Sanctuary*. In *Frank McGuinness Plays 2*, 265–342. London: Faber, 2002.

———. *Dolly West's Kitchen*. In *Frank McGuinness Plays 2*, 171–263. London: Faber, 2002.

———. *Gates of Gold*. London: Faber and Faber, 2002.

———. *Innocence: The Life and Death of Michelangelo Merisi, Caravaggio*. In *Frank McGuinness Plays 1*, 199–289. London: Faber, 1996.

———. "Masks." Introduction to *The Dazzling Dark*, ed. Frank McGuinness, ix–xii. London: Faber, 1996.

McManus, Antonia. *The Irish Hedge School and Its Books, 1695–1831*. Dublin: Four Courts Press, 2002.

McPherson, Conor. "Author's Note." *This Lime Tree Bower: Three Plays*. Dublin: New Island Books, 1996.

———. "Conor McPherson on *The Seafarer*." Abbey Theatre website. www.abbeytheatre.ie/literary/article/conor_mcpherson_on_the_seafarer (accessed March 8, 2010).

———. "If you're a young Irish playwright, come to London . . ." *New Statesman* 11, no. 492 (February 20, 1998): 38–41.

———. "An Interview with Connor McPherson." http://www.thelowry.com/Shows/seafarer.html (accessed April 8, 2007).

———. "Late Nights and Proclamations: The playwright recounts the beginnings of *The Weir*." *American Theatre* (April 1999): 45–46.

———. "So there's these three Irishmen." Interview with Tim Adams. *Sunday Observer*, February 4, 2001. http://observer.guardian.co.uk/review/story/0,,432996,00.html (accessed July 15, 2005).

———. *The Weir*. London: Nick Hern, 1998.

Meaney, Gerardine. *Gender, Ireland, and Cultural Change: Race, Sex, and Nation*. London: Routledge, 2010.

Mercier, Vivian. *The Irish Comic Tradition*. Oxford, UK: Clarendon Press, 1962.

Meredith, Dianne. "Landscape or Mindscape? Seamus Heaney's Bogs." *Irish Geography* 32, no. 2 (1999): 126–34.

Merriman, Vic. "Decolonization Postponed: The Theatre of Tiger Trash." *Irish University Review* 24, no. 2 (Autumn/Winter 1999): 305–17.

Mitchell, Frank, and Michael Ryan. *Reading the Irish Landscape*. Dublin: Town House Press, 1993.

Montague, John. *The Rough Field*. Newcastle upon Tyne, UK: Bloodaxe, 1990.

Morse, Donald, Csilla Bertha, and Mária Kurdi, eds. *Brian Friel's Dramatic Artistry: "The Work Has Value."* Dublin: Carysfort Press, 2006.

Murphy, Paula. "Staging Histories in Marina Carr's Midlands Plays." *Irish University Review* 36, no. 2 (September 2006): 389–403.

Murray, Christopher, ed. *Brian Friel: Essays, Diaries, Interviews: 1964–1999.* New York: Faber and Faber, 1999.

———. *Twentieth-Century Irish Drama: Mirror up to Nation.* Manchester, UK: Manchester UP, 1997.

Mustan, Munira H., and Laura P. Z. Izasrra. *Kaleidoscopic Views of Ireland.* São Paulo: U de São Paulo P, 2003.

Myth Busters: Deconstructing Myths about the Travelling Community. DivX film. Produced by Blanchardstown Traveller Development Group, in conjunction with "Know Racism" (Irish Anti-Racism Awareness Programme). 2005.

Nash, Catherine. "Reclaiming Vision: Looking at Landscape and the Body." *Gender, Place and Culture: A Journal of Feminist Geography* 3, no. 2 (1996): 149–69.

———. "Remapping and Renaming: New Cartographies of Identity, Gender and Landscape in Ireland." *Feminist Review* 44 (Summer 1993): 39–57.

Ni Anluain, Cliodhna, ed. *Reading the Future: Twelve Writers from Ireland in Conversation with Mike Murphy.* Dublin: Lilliput, 2000.

Ó Cadhla, Stiofán. *Civilizing Ireland: Ordnance Survey 1824–1842: Ethnography, Cartography, Translation.* Dublin: Irish Academic Press, 2007.

O'Connor, Frank. *The Lonely Voice: A Study of the Short Story.* Cleveland: World Publishing, 1963.

O'Toole, Fintan. "Hostility to Travellers Challenges Migratory Irish." *Irish Times,* June 16, 1995. 16.

———. "Shadows over Ireland." *American Theatre* 15 (July/August 1998): 18–19.

Relph, Edward. *Place and Placelessness.* London: Pion Limited, 1976.

Richards, Shaun, ed. *Twentieth-Century Irish Drama.* Cambridge: Cambridge UP, 2004.

Roche, Anthony. *Contemporary Irish Drama: From Beckett to McGuinness.* Dublin: Gill and Macmillan, 1994.

Rose, Gillian. *Feminism and Geography: The Limits of Geographical Knowledge.* Minneapolis: U of Minnesota P, 1993.

Rothstein, Mervyn. "The Subject Is Fear and the Excess It Breeds." Review of *Dublin Carol. New York Times*, February 16, 2003, AR7.

Roy, James Charles. "Landscape and the Celtic Soul." *Éire-Ireland* 31, no. 3 (Fall/Winter 1997): 228–54.

Rozik, Eli. *Generating Theatre Meaning: A Theory and Methodology of Performance Analysis.* Brighton, UK: Sussex Academic Press, 2008.

Schama, Simon. *Landscape and Memory.* New York: Knopf, 1995.

Scolnicov, Hanna. *Woman's Theatrical Space.* Cambridge: Cambridge UP, 1994.

Sihra, Melissa, ed. *Women in Irish Drama: A Century of Authorship and Representation.* New York: Palgrave Macmillan, 2007.

Sihra, Melissa, and Paul Murphy, eds. *The Dreaming Body: Contemporary Irish Theatre*. Gerrards Cross, UK: Colin Smythe, 2009.

Singleton, Brian. "Notes from a New Country." *Irish Theatre Magazine* 30 (2007): 58–61.

Smyth, Gerry. *Space and the Irish Cultural Imagination*. New York: Palgrave Macmillan, 2001.

Smyth, William J. *Map-making, Landscapes and Memory: A Geography of Colonial and Early Modern Ireland c. 1530–1750*. Cork: Cork UP, 2006.

Sontag, Susan. *On Photography*. New York: Farrar, Straus and Giroux, 1977.

Sullivan, Garrett A., Jr. *The Drama of Landscape: Land, Property, and Social Relations on the Early Modern Stage*. Stanford, CA: Stanford UP, 1998.

Synge, J. M. *Wicklow, West Kerry and Connemara* (1910). Totowa, NY: Rowman and Littlefield, 1980.

Thomas, Conor. *Colonialism's Culture: Anthropology, Travel, and Government*. Princeton, NJ: Princeton UP, 1994.

Wall, Cynthia. "Gendering Rooms: Domestic Architecture and Literary Acts." *Eighteenth-Century Fiction* 5, no.4 (July 1993): 333–72.

Wall, Wendy. *Staging Domesticity: Household Work and English Identity in Early Modern Drama*. Cambridge: Cambridge UP, 2002.

Walshe, Éibhear, ed. *Sex, Nation, and Dissent in Irish Writing*. Cork: Cork UP, 1997.

White, Victoria. "Telling Stories in the Dark." *Irish Times*, July 2, 1998.

Wilson, Elizabeth. *The Sphinx in the City: Urban Life, the Control of Disorder, and Women.* Berkeley, CA: U of California P, 1991.

Wood, Gerald C. *Conor McPherson: Imagining Mischief.* Dublin: Liffey Press, 2003.

Index

Abbey Theatre, 2, 12, 21, 23, 39, 49, 69, 82, 121, 127, 131, 142n, 144n, 146n, 151n, 163n, 165n
Ambassadors Theatre, 52
"American Wake," 3, 114
Andrews, J. H., 18, 26, 137n, 141n, 143n
Ardener, Shirley, 150n
Arnaud, Noel, 97
Arnold, Matthew, 86
Aron, Geraldine, 111
Artaud, Antonin, 1, 4, 128
Ascendency, 69
audience, 1–2, 4–9, 11–13, 16–17, 24, 29, 33, 36, 39–44, 50, 52–54, 57, 65–68, 70, 72, 74–76, 82–83, 85, 89, 92–93, 95, 98–100, 102–4, 107–9, 113, 115–23, 125, 128–29, 131–32, 142n, 145n, 146n, 151n, 157n
Ayckbourn, Alan, 101, 103

Bachelard, Gaston, 97, 115, 116
Balleybeg, 36
bar, 38, 40–44, 46–49, 51–57, 59–63, 131, 143n. *See also* pub
Barthes, Roland, 84
Baudelaire, Charles, 103
Beckett, Samuel, 2, 11–12, 31, 59, 87, 94, 108, 141n
  Act Without Words I, 151n
  Eh, Joe, 155n
  Footfalls, 155n
  Happy Days, 151n
  Quad, Quadrat, 11, 108
  Rough for Theatre I, 151n
  Waiting for Godot, 151n
bedroom, 99, 106–10, 118–22, 124–25, 131, 156n. *See also* beds/bed space
beds/bed space, 106, 110–11, 119, 122–25, 155n
Belfast, 12, 138n, 145n

belong/belonging, 1, 8, 9, 11, 13, 16–18, 23, 27–28, 30–32, 35–36, 38, 41, 49–53, 57, 61, 65, 67, 71–72, 74, 77, 80, 84–86, 88–90, 93–95, 101, 109–12, 113–16, 118, 120, 122–27, 130–32, 150n, 152n
Bentley, Eric, 130
Bertha, Csilla, 100
big house, 69
bogs, 10–11, 65–75, 78–83, 85–92, 95, 124, 131, 149n, 157n
books, 16, 17, 140n
Boone, Joseph Allen, 120–21
Booterstown Marsh, 105
borders, 8, 19, 23, 35, 81, 87, 88, 95, 136n. *See also* boundaries
Borges, Jorge Luis, 142n
boundaries, 15, 28, 29, 35, 59, 75, 81, 88, 99, 120, 121, 124. *See also* borders
Burke, Mary, 82, 89, 148n, 149n

"camp"/"camping," 111, 120
campers/campsites, 43, 61, 74, 110, 111
caravan, 70, 74, 78, 82, 90, 94
Carleton, William, 32, 139n

Carr, Marina, 5, 11, 65–96, 98, 118, 124, 145n, 146n, 149n, 150n, 152n, 153n
Ariel, 66
By the Bog of Cats…, 13, 19, 44, 47, 65–96, 98, 102, 106, 113, 118, 119, 125, 157n
Low in the Dark, 83
Mai, The, 66, 87, 145n
Portia Coughlin, 66
On Raftery's Hill, 66, 85
Carroll, Lewis, 141n
Carthage (town), 81–82
cartography/cartographer, 20, 21, 29, 32, 34
Cashman, John, 46
Catholicism, 56. *See also* priests
Celtic Tiger, 3, 48, 82, 94
Cerquoni, Enrica, 77
Charabanc Theatre Company, 12
Chaudhuri, Una, 3, 4, 98, 129, 144n
Chekhov, Anton, 17, 63, 137n
children, 12, 36, 62, 72, 77, 84, 95, 119, 127, 129. *See also* family
city, 54, 55, 60, 77, 101, 109, 115, 119, 131. *See also* urban

clothing, 84, 85. *See also* fashion
colonial, post-colonial, colonialism, 7, 11, 16, 17, 19, 23, 29, 30, 31, 33, 34, 76, 81, 82, 86
Colum, Padraic, 139n
constitution, Irish, 23, 78, 145n, 150n
Convictions, 12
cottage, 9–11, 17, 40, 69, 100, 102–3, 127, 138n
Coward, Noel, 101, 103
Cregan, David, 111
Crumlin Road, 12

Deane, Seamus, 2, 43, 65, 149n
Dedalus, Stephen, 13
Derrida, Jacques, 153n
Derry City, 11, 112, 136n
de Valera, Eamon, 40, 139n
dialect, 47, 68, 100, 146n. *See also* Irish English
Diceman, 12
Dickens, Charles, 83
dinnseanchas, 25, 28, 30, 36, 71
Donegal, 11, 15, 18–19, 20–23, 30, 34–35, 39, 98, 112, 132–33
Dowling, P. J., 24, 27, 140n

Dublin, 11–13, 19, 23, 39, 41, 45, 50, 55, 59, 68, 97–99, 115, 119, 121, 124
Duffy, Patrick, 40, 48, 138n

Eat the Peach, 67
Edwards, Hilton, 90, 100–104, 115–16, 121–22, 126, 154n
Elam, Keir, 151n
Electricity Supply Board (ESB): 38, 41, 44–46
Eliot, T. S., 4
Elizabethan stage, 8, 103–4
emigrant/emigration, 3, 114, 127, 129
"Emigrant Wake." *See* "American Wake"
Entrikin, J. Nicholas, 28, 60
European Union, 41, 46, 93, 147n
exile, 1–3, 13, 87, 98, 113–14, 118, 120, 125

Fáilte Ireland, 45
fairies, 30, 53, 56–59, 61–62
Fall of the House of Usher, The, 58
family, 17, 22, 27–28, 36, 50, 59–60, 62–63, 65, 71, 73, 80, 90, 95, 97, 103, 112, 119, 125, 132, 152n
famine, 27

fashion, 84. *See also* clothing
Fischer-Lichte, Erika, 4, 6
flâneur/flâneuse, 77
Foley, Imelda, 111
Ford, John, 66
  Quiet Man, The, 66
Foster, John Wilson, 47, 73, 141n
Foucault, Michel, 109, 111, 119, 156n
  History of Sexuality, The, 109
Fouéré, Olwen, 82–83, 146n, 150n
fourth wall, 52
Frawley, Monica, 82
Friel, Brian, 2, 11, 15–36, 45, 50, 74–75, 95, 98, 100, 102, 110, 112–13, 116, 123–24, 137n, 139n, 142n, 143n, 155n
  Dancing at Lughnasa, 75
  Faith Healer, 155n
  Gentle Island, The, 139n
  Philadelphia, Here I Come!, 95, 100, 110, 118, 123
  Translations, 2, 11, 13, 15–36, 41, 53, 61, 74, 76, 95, 102, 113, 119, 124–25, 133, 136n, 139n, 140n
  Wonderful Tennessee, 45, 50, 142n, 143n, 155n

Gaelic. *See* Irish language
Gate Theatre, 37, 40, 50, 99, 103–4, 108, 115, 119, 121, 157n
gay. *See* homosexuality
ghost(s), 45, 49–50, 56, 58, 63, 66–67, 71–72, 74–75, 81, 85–86, 88–89, 94
Ghost Fancier, 72, 81, 94, 145n
Gleitman, Claire, 113
globalization, 4, 32, 41, 62, 130
Gluckstein, Hannah (Gluck), 104
gombeenism, 99
Greece/Greek, 8, 16, 22, 29, 139n
Greek drama, 76–77, 103–4, 145n, 149n
Gregory, Lady Augusta, 148n
Grene, Nicholas, 8, 48, 112, 128, 146n
Guildhall, Derry, 11

Hawkes, Terence, 35
Hawthorne, Nathaniel, 76, 79, 150n
  Scarlet Letter, The, 76, 79, 150n
Hayes, Michael, 148n, 152n, 153n

Heaney, Seamus, 9, 22, 25, 74, 76, 123, 140n, 141n, 149n
hedge school, 16–17, 19, 21–22, 24, 27, 29–30, 32, 34, 139n, 140n, 141n
Henry, Paul, 22, 39, 55, 138n
Heritage Council, 45
Hirsch, Edward, 23
home/homeland, 1, 3, 7–10, 12–13, 16–20, 22–24, 32, 36–38, 41, 43–44, 46–48, 50–52, 54–57, 60–62, 65–66, 68, 73, 77–80, 89, 93–95, 97–105, 110–15, 117–18, 120, 122–26, 127–33
Homer, 22
homosexual/homosexuality, 111, 124. See also gay
Hornby, Richard, 6
Hughes, Declan, 11, 100
Hynes, Garry, 50, 67, 127

Ibsen, Henrik, 77, 95, 102, 123–24
Doll's House, A, 95, 102, 104
Hedda Gabbler, 104
immigration, 94
Into the West, 68

Irish language, 18, 26, 36, 47, 137n, 140n
Issacharoff, Michael, 136n
itinerants. *See* Travellers
I Went Down, 67

Jackson, John Brinckerhoff, 138n
Johnson, Matthew, 25, 48
Jordan, Eamonn, 11, 57, 149n
Joyce, James, 120, 156n
  Dubliners, 156n
  Finnegan's Wake, 156n
  Portrait of the Artist as a Young Man, A, 13, 38
  Ulysses, 120

Keane, J. B., 12, 44, 90
  Field, The, 12, 44, 90
  Sive, 12
Keating, Sean, 45
Kiberd, Declan, 18, 32, 115
Klein, Bernhard, 20
Kolodny, Annette, 78

landscape, 8, 15, 18–20, 25, 27–28, 32, 34, 37–64, 66, 68, 78, 82–83, 86–87, 89, 95, 98, 104, 106, 123, 130, 132, 138n
Lanters, José, 88

Lefebvre, Henri, 6, 31, 65, 88, 99, 108–9, 125
Leitrim, 37–39, 50, 55, 61
liminal/liminality, 8, 43, 66
Lonergan, Patrick, ix, 8, 32, 83, 131–32
Lorca, Federico Garcia, 101
House of Bernarda Alba, The, 101

MacLíammóir, Micheál, 99–104, 115–16, 120–22, 125–26, 154n
Magritte, René, 42, 106
La Condition Humaine, 42, 106
Mamet, David, 47
maps/mapping, 15–36, 52, 68, 76–77, 124, 131–33, 137n, 141n
Martinovich, M. K., 77
Mason, Patrick, 131
McAuley, Gay, 6
McGuinness, Frank, 11–12, 72, 75, 82, 95, 97–126, 131–32, 146n, 148n, 154n, 155n
Bird Sanctuary, The, 75–76, 105–6, 117, 121
Bread Man, The, 112
Carthaginians, 82, 95, 110, 112–13, 117, 122

Dolly West's Kitchen, 75, 95, 113, 116–17, 132
Factory Girls, The, 103, 110, 122
Gates of Gold, 12–13, 72, 97–126, 131
Innocence, 113, 117, 121
Mary and Lizzie, 113
Mutabilitie, 101, 113, 137n, 148n
Observe the Sons of Ulster Marching Towards the Somme, 101, 109–10, 112, 116, 122
Someone Who'll Watch Over Me, 103, 109, 112, 115, 122
There Came a Gypsy Riding, 110, 113, 116, 156n
McPherson, Conor, 11, 37–63, 67, 75, 98, 104, 157n
I Went Down, 67
Seafarer, The, 52
Weir, The, 13, 19, 37–63, 76, 84, 93, 102, 104–5, 107, 125, 157n
Medea, 76, 82, 149n
Midlands, 11, 65, 67–69, 92–95, 152n
mirror(s), 106, 109, 111, 120–21, 155n

modernism, 9, 46, 97
Montague, John, 47
Morrison, Kristen, 59
Mother Ireland, 150n
Murphy, Paula, 92
Murphy, Tom, 123, 148n, 155n
  Bailegangaire, 123
Murray, Christopher, 141n
music, 51, 66–67, 75, 91, 103, 113–14, 119, 156n

National Education Board, 29, 141n
Nora. *See* Synge, J. M.; Ibsen, Henrik

O'Casey, Sean, 102–3
O'Connor, Frank, 93
O'Hara, Maureen, 66
O'Neill, Eugene, 108
Ordnance Survey, 18, 33–34, 35–36, 137n
orthography/orthographer, 15, 26, 34
O'Toole, Fintan, 130, 148n

paintings, 42, 45, 47, 76, 104–6, 138n. *See also* Magritte, René

photographs, 38, 40–45, 48–50, 76, 84, 105, 143n. *See also* Sontag, Susan
potato famine, 27
priests, 56–58, 61, 140n. *See also* Catholicism
Prynne, Hester. *See* Hawthorne, Nathaniel
pub, 18, 38–40, 61, 143n

queer. *See* homosexuality

Relph, Edward, 15
Riches, The, 152n
Rickson, Ian, 48
Roche, Anthony, 101, 131
Rocky Horror Picture Show, The, 12
Rose, Gillian, 78, 118, 123
Rotunda Hospital, 12, 119
Roy, James Charles, 92
Royal Court Theatre, 50, 52
Rozik, Eli, 2, 4, 67, 72
rural, 6, 11, 13, 17, 19, 22–23, 30, 37, 39–41, 43–45, 47–48, 50–51, 54–55, 57, 66, 68, 94, 97–100, 104–5, 113, 126–27, 130, 132, 138n, 139n, 140n, 143n, 145n
Rural Electrification Scheme, 40, 44

sappers, 17, 25
Scolnicov, Hanna, 77
Shakespeare, 5, 15, 20, 26, 103
   Comedy of Errors, The, 137n
   Hamlet, 58, 72
   King Lear, 15, 35
   Macbeth, 67, 81
   Merchant of Venice, The, 5
   Taming of the Shrew, The, 5
Shakespearean stage. *See* Elizabethan stage
Shannon River, 38, 40, 44–45, 157n
Sihra, Melissa, 95
Sligo, 37
Smith, Rae, 52
Smyth, Gerry, 55
songs. *See* music
Sontag, Susan, 42
split stage, 101, 107–8
Spring Rice Report, 33
standardization, 17, 21, 74
Steiner, George, 18, 27
Stembridge, Gerard, 111
stereotypes, 73, 76, 78, 80, 92, 111, 116–17, 127, 152n
stories/storytelling, 38–39, 43, 46, 48–49, 53–54, 56–59, 61–63, 131
Strange Brew, 58
Strindberg, August, 110
Sullivan, Garrett A., 35

survey, surveyor, 17–18, 20, 26–30, 32–36, 48, 61, 124
Synge, J. M., 19, 23, 40, 47, 49, 51, 55, 75, 77, 94–95, 103, 113, 145n

tinker, 69–71, 81–82, 88–90, 92, 148n
tourists/tourism, 12–13, 20, 39–44, 46–47, 51–52, 55, 60–61, 63, 127
translation/translator, 15–36, 100, 140n
Traveller, 66, 68–73, 77, 88–94, 118, 130, 147n, 148n, 149n, 151n, 152n, 153n
Turner, Victor, 8
Turn of the Screw, The, 58

Ulster, 9–10
Ulysses, 22
urban, 5–6, 13, 19, 23, 30, 39–41, 44, 50, 54–55, 58, 60, 62–63, 68, 77, 98–100, 102, 104–5, 109, 115, 125–26, 130, 133, 143n, 145n, 150n

Virgil, 22

Walton, J. Michael, 77
weddings, 8, 67, 80–85, 87–88, 92, 106

Williams, Tennessee, 104, 108
  Glass Menagerie, The, 104
  Streetcar Named Desire, A, 108
windows, 19, 25, 34, 41–42,
  99, 106, 116
women, 55, 57, 62–63, 73,
  76–81, 83–86, 89, 92,
  126, 148n, 150n

Wordsworth, William, 24,
  48, 74
  "Lines: Composed a Few
    Miles above Tintern
    Abbey," 48, 74

Yeats, William Butler,
  40, 47

GPSR Compliance

The European Union's (EU) General Product Safety Regulation (GPSR) is a set of rules that requires consumer products to be safe and our obligations to ensure this.

If you have any concerns about our products, you can contact us on

ProductSafety@springernature.com

In case Publisher is established outside the EU, the EU authorized representative is:

Springer Nature Customer Service Center GmbH
Europaplatz 3
69115 Heidelberg, Germany

www.ingramcontent.com/pod-product-compliance
Lightning Source LLC
LaVergne TN
LVHW051911060526
838200LV00004B/94